CATECHISM FOR CHILDREN

CATECHISM FOR CHILDREN

CATECHISM FOR ENGLISH-SPEAKING DIOCESES

By Canon Quinet
General Secretary of the National Catechism
Commission, Honorary Inspector
of Religious Education of the Diocese of Paris

and Canon Boyer
Director of the National Catechetic Center,
Director of Religious Education
of the Diocese of Dijon

Translated by Miss Ann Marie Temple

2915 Forest Avenue | Kansas City, MO 64109

©2012 by Angelus Press
All rights reserved. No part of this book may be reproduced or transmitted in any form or by any means, electronic or mechanical, including photocopying, recording, or by any information storage and retrieval systems without permission in writing from the publisher, except by a reviewer, who may quote brief passages in a review.

ANGELUS PRESS
2915 FOREST AVENUE
KANSAS CITY, MISSOURI 64109
PHONE (816) 753-3150
FAX (816) 753-3557
ORDER LINE 1-800-966-7337
www.angeluspress.org

ISBN 978-1-937843-07-6
FIRST PRINTING–August 2012
SECOND PRINTING–September 2014

Printed in the United States of America

CONTENTS

Foreword viii
Morning Prayer 1
Evening Prayer 3
The Catechism 5
The Prayer of a Christian 8

PART 1: The Truths Which Jesus Christ Taught Us

1. The Apostles' Creed 13
2. God Exists 18
3. The Nature and Perfection of God 22
4. The Mysteries of Religion 27
5. Mystery of the Holy Trinity 31
6. Angels and Devils 36
7. The Creation of Man 40
8. Original Sin 44
9. The Mystery of the Incarnation 63
10. The Mystery of the Incarnation (continued) 67
11. The Childhood and the Youth of Our
    Lord Jesus Christ 72
12. The Public Life of Our Lord 77
13. Our Lord Jesus Christ is God 81
14. The Mystery of the Redemption 86
15. The Resurrection of Our Lord Jesus Christ . . . 93
16. The Ascension 97
17. The Holy Ghost 101
18. The Church 108
19. The Hierarchy of the Church 112
20. The Marks of the True Church 117
21. The Faithful of the Church 123
22. The Communion of Saints 127
23. The Forgiveness of Sins 132
24. Life Everlasting 136

PART 2: The Remedies Which Jesus Christ Prepared for Us

25. Grace in General 143
    I. Sanctifying Grace. 143
26. II. Actual Grace 148
27. Prayer 152
28. The Our Father 156
29. The Angelic Salutation 160
30. The Sacraments. 165
31. Baptism 170
32. Confirmation 175
33. The Eucharist 180
34. The Holy Sacrifice of the Mass 187
35. Holy Communion 194
36. How to Receive Communion Well 198
37. Penance 203
38. Contrition 208
39. Confession 213
40. The Manner of Going to Confession 217
41. Satisfaction or Reparation 222
42. Extreme Unction 226
43. Holy Orders 231
44. I. Matrimony 236
45. II. The Conditions of Matrimony 239

PART 3: The Commandments Which Jesus Christ Gave to Us

46. The Commandments 245
47. The Virtues 251
48. The Theological Virtues. 256
    I. The Virtue of Faith 256
49. II. The Virtue of Hope 260
50. III. The Virtue of Charity. 264
    A. The Love of God 264

Contents

51. B. The Love of Neighbor 268
52. The First Commandment of God 273
    I. The Worship Due to God
    and to Jesus Christ 273
53. The First Commandment of God (continued) . 278
    II. The Devotion Due to the Blessed Virgin
    and to the Saints 278
54. The Second Commandment of God 283
55. The Third Commandment of God 287
56. The Fourth Commandment of God 291
    I. Duties of Children
    Toward Their Parents 291
    II. Duties of Parents
    Toward Their Children 294
57. The Fourth Commandment of God (Continued) 297
    III. Duties Toward One's
    Homeland and Toward All Men 297
58. The Fifth Commandment of God 301
59. The Sixth and Ninth Commandments of God . 307
60. The Seventh and Tenth Commandments of God 312
61. The Eighth Commandment of God 317
62. The Precepts of the Church 322
63. Sin 329
64. The Vices or Capital Sins 333
65. The Day of a Christian 334
66. Revelation and the Bible 344
67. The Holy Bible 347

    Prayers 349
    The Rosary 359
    Visit to the Most Blessed Sacrament 362
    The Sacrament of Penance 364
    The Holy Sacrifice of the Mass 371

Foreword

A cross (†) indicates questions for 2nd and 3rd grade students.

A dot (•) indicates questions for 4th and 5th grade students.

All other questions are for students of the higher grades.

Each chapter begins with an illustrated Gospel story meant to prepare the student to assimilate the lesson. This story is followed by a short series of review questions and then the lesson itself.

Immediately after the lesson comes an application: "**For my life**," designed to integrate the lesson immediately into the life of the child; a prayer in accordance with that application; a text from Holy Scripture: "**The Word of God**," with a pedagogical sketch, providing a synthesis of the chapter as a whole.

Next, we have included a note on the liturgy connected with the chapter studied, a homework assignment and suggestions for independent work. They can be useful for extending catechism teaching to the home, under a different form.

Morning Prayer

✠ In the Name of the Father and of the Son and of the Holy Ghost. Amen.

Place yourself in the presence of God and adore Him.

Most Holy Trinity, one God in three Persons, I believe that You are present here with me. I adore You with the very deepest humility and with all of my heart I offer You the worship due to Your sovereign Majesty.

My God, I very humbly thank You for all of the graces which You have granted to me up to this moment. It is again through Your goodness that I am here to see this day, and so I wish to make use of it only to serve You. I CONSECRATE TO YOU ALL OF MY THOUGHTS, WORDS, ACTIONS, AND SUFFERINGS OF THIS DAY. Bless them, my Lord, in order that every single one of them might be animated by Your love and tend toward Your greater glory.

Divine Heart of Jesus, I offer You, through the Immaculate Heart of Mary, my prayers, works and sufferings of this day, in reparation for offenses, and for all of the intentions for which You immolate Yourself continually upon the altar.

Act of Faith

O my God, I firmly believe that Thou art one God in three divine Persons, the Father, the Son, and the Holy Ghost. I believe that Thy divine Son became Man, and died for our sins, and that He will come to judge the living and the dead. I believe these and all the truths which the holy Catholic Church teaches, because Thou hast revealed them, Who canst neither deceive nor be deceived.

Act of Hope

O my God, relying on Thy infinite goodness and promises, I hope to obtain pardon of my sins, the help of Thy grace, and life everlasting, through the merits of Jesus Christ, my Lord and Redeemer.

Act of Charity

O my God, I love Thee above all things, with my whole heart and soul, because Thou art all good and worthy of all love. I love my neighbor as myself for love of Thee. I forgive all who have injured me and ask pardon of all whom I have injured.

O Mary, conceived without sin, pray for us who have recourse to thee.

EVENING PRAYER

✠ In the Name of the Father and of the Son and of the Holy Ghost. Amen.

Place yourself in the presence of God and adore Him.

I adore You, my God. I believe that You love me and I thank You for all of the graces which You have showered upon me during this day. Thank You for this new day; thank You for having given me a family. Thank You for the good which You have allowed me to do; thank You for protecting me.

I ask forgiveness for all of the sins which I have committed against You.

Make an EXAMINATION OF CONSCIENCE, which means: try to remember all of the sins which you committed during the day:

- against God
- against your neighbor (other people)
- against yourself

ACT OF CONTRITION

O my God, I am heartily sorry for having offended Thee, and I detest all my sins because I dread the loss of heaven and the pains of hell, but most of all because they offend Thee, my God, Who art all good and deserving of all my love. I firmly resolve with the help of Thy grace, to confess my sins, to do penance, and to amend my life. Amen.

Say:

1 Our Father, 3 Hail Marys, 1 Glory Be,

or better yet:

1 decade of the rosary (*1 Our Father, 10 Hail Marys, 1 Glory Be*).

Bless, my God, the rest which I am about to take in order to regain my strength, that I might serve You better. Holy Virgin, Mother of my God and after Him my only Hope, my good Angel, my patron saint, intercede for me, protect me during this night, throughout all of my life and at the hour of my death. Amen.

Reminder of the prayer "Glory Be"

Glory be to the Father and to the Son and to the Holy Ghost, as it was in the beginning, is now and ever shall be, world without end. Amen.

Introductory Lesson (Part 1)

The Catechism

Around the year 42, the inhabitants of the town of Antioch gave the name of "Christians" to those who believed in Christ and who had received Baptism.

We now apply the same name to all those who are members of the Christian religion. You, too, are Christian, because you have been baptized, and you are Catholic because you are a child of the Church whose head is the Pope. But you should not only have the name of Christian, you should believe what Christ taught, do what He commanded, and make use of all of the means which He placed at your disposal in order to be a good Christian.

If you do all of these things, you will be united to Jesus the way a disciple is united to his master, and you will develop the life of God given to your soul by Baptism.

The Catechism, this little book which you are holding in your hands, will be like a guide for you which will lead you to the happiness of heaven.

Love your catechism, think of it as the most useful and the most necessary book you own.

REVIEW – Where does the name of "Christian" come from? – Why are you called a Christian? – Why are you called a Catholic? – What should you do in order to be a good Christian? – By being a good Christian, what life will you be developing in your soul? – Why should you love your catechism?

LESSON

• 1. *What is the catechism?*

The catechism is a summary of the religion revealed by God.

† 2. *What does religion teach you?*

Religion teaches us to know God, what He has done for us, and the means for going to heaven.

3. *What is the true religion?*

The true religion is the Catholic religion, revealed by God, taught by His own Son Jesus Christ, and handed down through the Catholic Church.

4. *What must you do to merit Heaven?*

To merit Heaven:
- 1st **I must believe the truths which Jesus Christ has taught us;**
- 2nd **I must do good and avoid evil for love of Jesus Christ;**
- 3rd **I must pray every day and use the means by which Jesus Christ wants to strengthen me to be faithful.**

5. *What is a Christian?*

A Christian is one who is baptized and who follows faithfully the teaching of Jesus.

6. *What does the catechism include?*

The catechism includes:
- **1st   the truths which Jesus Christ taught us;**
- **2nd   the helps which Jesus Christ prepared for us;**
- **3rd   the commandments which Jesus Christ gave us.**

FOR MY LIFE – Catechism class is where I am supposed to learn the meaning of my life and the way to find true happiness. That is why I will pay attention to the teaching given to me there, and why I will carefully study each lesson.

PRAYER – My God, give us the graces which are necessary for us to learn our catechism well, to understand it well and to live it well, so that we might better know You, love You and serve You every single day.

THE WORD OF GOD – "Blessed are they who hear the word of God and keep it." (Luke 11:28)

INTRODUCTORY LESSON (PART 2)

THE PRAYER OF A CHRISTIAN

Jesus asks us to pray. He gave us the example, for often He went away alone at night to pray.

One day Our Lord spoke to His disciples about prayer, and He said to them: "When thou shalt pray, enter into thy chamber, and having shut the door, pray to thy Father in secret, and thy Father Who seeth in secret will repay thee."[1]

He also told us to pray together: "For where there are two or three gathered together in My Name, there am I in the midst of them."[2]

We should pray morning and evening, and in all important circumstances. It is normal to say family prayers. Pope Pius XII said: "A praying family is a living family."

---

[1] Matthew 6:6
[2] Matthew 18:20

THE PRAYER OF A CHRISTIAN

LESSON

† 7. *What is prayer?*

Prayer is speaking to God, as a child speaks to his Father in heaven.

• 8. *Are we obliged to pray?*

Yes, we are obliged to pray every day. Jesus often says so in the Gospel.

9. *What is the normal position for morning and evening prayer?*

I should normally pray on my knees, before a Crucifix, with respect and love of God.

† 10. *How do we begin and end a prayer?*

We begin and end a prayer by the sign of the cross.

• 11. *How do you make the sign of the cross?*

I make the sign of the cross by bringing my right hand to my forehead and saying: In the Name of the Father; then to my chest, saying: and of the Son; then to my left shoulder and my right shoulder, saying: and of the Holy Ghost; at the end I say: Amen.

† 12. *What is the most beautiful of all prayers?*

The most beautiful of all prayers is the one which Jesus Christ Himself taught to us:

"Our Father, Who art in heaven, hallowed be Thy Name; Thy kingdom come, Thy will be done, on earth as it is in heaven.

"Give us this day our daily bread, and forgive us our trespasses as we forgive those who trespass against us; and lead us not into temptation, but deliver us from evil. Amen."

† 13. *What is another prayer that Christians say with the greatest confidence?*

"Hail Mary, full of grace, the Lord is with thee. Blessed art thou among women, and blessed is the fruit of thy womb, Jesus.

"Holy Mary, Mother of God, pray for us sinners, now and at the hour of our death. Amen."

14. *What should you always add to your evening prayer?*

Every evening, I should look into my soul and try to remember the sins of that day, and ask God to forgive me for them. This is the examination of conscience.

FOR MY LIFE – A Christian family says its prayers together. I will ask my parents, my brothers and my sisters if they want to say them with me.

THE WORD OF GOD – "For where there are two or three gathered together in My Name, there am I in the midst of them." (Matthew 18:20)

FIRST PART

The Truths Which Jesus Christ Taught Us

Jesus Christ Said: "I Am…**THE TRUTH**…"

"He who listens to My word and believes in Him Who sent Me will have eternal Life."

Lesson 1

The Apostles' Creed

You know by heart the "I believe in God." It is a prayer which is the affirmation of your faith. You say: I believe in God. It is also a story which reminds us that God the Father created everything, that God the Son saved us, and that the Holy Ghost made us children of God. In the whole first part of the Catechism you are going to study this wonderful story in detail.

But where does the Creed come from? It comes to us from the Apostles, as its name indicates. It is the summary of their teaching.

You know who the Apostles were: twelve men whom Jesus chose, and to whom He gave His teaching over a period of three years. He had chosen them from among the laborers. Some were fishermen like Peter, James and John.

One day Jesus climbed into Peter's fishing boat and said to him: "Launch out into the deep and let down your nets for a draught." – Peter answered, "Master, we have labored all the night and have taken nothing, but at Thy word I will let down the net."

He did well because when he cast out his nets, they were so full of fish that he had to call two other fishermen to help him pull them out of the water. That is when Jesus said to him: "Fear not: from henceforth thou shalt catch men."[3] Peter was to become the head of the Apostles.

REVIEW – How is the "I believe in God" a prayer? – How is it a story? – In what part of the catechism will you study it in detail? – Where does this prayer come from? – From among what sort of people did Jesus choose His Apostles? – Tell the story of the call of Peter.

LESSON

- 15. *What are the truths that you must believe?*

The truths I must believe are those that Jesus Christ has made known, and that He teaches through His Church.

16. *Why must you believe the truths which the Church teaches you?*

I must believe the truths which the Church teaches me because it is Jesus Christ Who made them known, and He can neither deceive nor be deceived.

---

[3] Luke 5:4-11.

The Apostles' Creed

17. *When we believe the truths revealed by God, what sort of act are we making?*

When we believe the truths revealed by God we are making an act of Faith.

● 18. *Where do you find the principal truths which Jesus Christ has made known?*

I find the principal truths which Jesus Christ has made known in the Apostles' Creed.

19. *Who were the Apostles?*

The Apostles were twelve men chosen by Jesus Christ to preach His religion and continue His work.

† 20. *Recite the Apostles' Creed.*

1st **I believe in God the Father Almighty, Creator of heaven and earth;**
2nd **and in Jesus Christ, His only Son, Our Lord;**
3rd **Who was conceived by the Holy Ghost, born of the Virgin Mary,**
4th **suffered under Pontius Pilate, was crucified, died and was buried.**
5th **He descended into hell; the third day He rose again from the dead;**
6th **He ascended into heaven, sitteth at the right hand of God, the Father Almighty;**
7th **from thence He shall come to judge the living and the dead.**
8th **I believe in the Holy Ghost,**
9th **the Holy Catholic Church, the communion of saints,**

10th the forgiveness of sins,
11th the resurrection of the body,
12th and life everlasting. Amen.

> **FOR MY LIFE** – I will recite the Apostles' Creed every day, to tell God daily that I believe everything that it contains.
>
> **PRAYER** – I believe in God…
>
> **THE WORD OF GOD** – "Jesus said to the Apostles: 'Who hears you, hears Me.'" (Luke 10:16)

LITURGY – If one day you are asked to be a godparent, you will recite the "I believe in God" for the little baby about to be baptized.

ASSIGNMENT – What did the Apostles do to show that they believed what they taught? – Should not you, too, be an apostle? – How can you be an apostle among your friends? at home? in the parish?

PROJECT – Illustrate each article of the Creed with one or more pictures.

The Apostles uphold the Church the way pillars uphold the vault of a Cathedral

Almighty God, Creator of Heaven and Earth

Lesson 2

The First Article of the Creed

"I believe in God the Father Almighty, Creator of heaven and earth..."

God Exists

If someone said to you: "The book which you are holding in your hands put itself together all by itself; the letters lined themselves up in the right order to make a word; the words arranged themselves into sentences," you would say: "That is impossible; someone thought out this book, wrote it, then sent it to the printer, and the book was made, thanks to the work of men."

Look at the sea, the land, the mountains; see the stars in the sky, and remember that they all obey laws which you can study in your school books. Think about how the scholars tell us that the world has not always existed, and then ask yourself who made all these things; who wanted there to be a night, a day, seasons; who gave the earth the power to make seeds grow, and who gave the sun the power to make them ripen.

It is a Being of infinite power Whom we do not see but Who left His trace in everything that exists, just as the author of a book leaves the mark of his thought on all of the pages.

God has made Himself known to man by His works, yet He has also used other means. In Bible History we learn that He spoke to Adam and Eve, to the patriarchs, and to Moses – to whom He appeared in a bush that burned without being consumed.

You will soon see that it is above all in the Person of His Son, Our Lord Jesus Christ, that God has made Himself known.

REVIEW – Do you see the one who made this book? – Who printed it? – How was this book made? – Has the world always existed? – Who made the world? – Who gave laws to the universe? – To whom has God made Himself known?

LESSON

† 21. *What is God?*

God is a spirit, eternal and infinitely perfect, Creator and Master of all things.

• 22. *Why are you certain that there is a God?*

I am certain that there is a God because all of the creatures prove His existence.

> NOTE: Creatures prove that God exists, because they could not have made themselves. Reason tells us that if there had to be a worker in order for a house to be built, there had to be a Creator for heaven and earth to be made out of nothing.

23. *Have most peoples believed that God exists?*

Yes, most peoples have believed that God exists.

24. *Has God made Himself known to man?*

Yes, God made Himself known to the first men, then to Moses and the prophets; and above all, through His Son Jesus Christ.

† 25. *What did Jesus Christ say of God?*

Jesus Christ said that God is not only the Creator of all things, but the Father of all men.

GOD EXISTS

> **FOR MY LIFE** – God made everything out of nothing. He is the Master of everything.
>
> **PRAYER** – I believe in God...Creator of heaven and earth.
>
> **THE WORD OF GOD** – "The heavens show forth the glory of God." (Psalm 18:1)

LITURGY – In her official prayer, the Roman Church uses the Latin language for the worship of God. Latin is a universal language understood in all parts of the Church. However, in certain countries, they use other ancient languages.

In your prayer book, you have the translation next to the Latin.

ASSIGNMENT – Does not your calendar tell you the time of the rising and setting of the sun? – The dates of springtime, summer, autumn, winter? – Is the sun ever late, or are the phases of the moon? Why not? – Do you know of any machine as well built as the universe? Who made it?

PROJECT – Draw a beautiful map of the sky.

Lesson 3

The Nature and Perfection of God

When you recite the "I believe in God," you say: "I believe in God the Father almighty, Creator of heaven and earth…" You know what "I believe" means but you need to understand properly the word "Creator." It means He Who made out of nothing everything that exists: the sky with all its stars, the moon, the sun; the earth with all that it contains. God spoke, and everything was made. What is this God like?

Jesus is going to tell you: One day when He was sitting beside a well, a woman of Samaria came to draw water. In the conversation He had with this woman, Jesus told us what God is like: "God is a spirit," He said.[4] That means He is like your soul: we cannot see Him, we cannot touch Him. But just as your soul is everywhere in your body, so God is everywhere. It is this all-powerful God Who created us out of kindness

---

[4] John 4:24

and Who watches over us the way a father watches over his children.

In speaking of God's care for all of His creatures, Jesus said: "Behold the birds of the air, for they neither sow, nor do they reap, nor gather into barns: and your heavenly Father feedeth them. Are not you of much more value than they?...Be not solicitous, therefore....For your Father knoweth that you have need of these things....Consider the lilies of the field, how they grow: they labor not, neither do they spin. But I say to you, that not even Solomon in all his glory was arrayed as one of these. And if the grass of the field, which is today and tomorrow is cast into the oven, God doth so clothe: how much more you?"[5]

REVIEW – What does the word "creature" mean? – What did Jesus say to the Samaritan woman? – What do you understand by the word "spirit"? – Is God only a Master for us? – What does Jesus say in speaking of God's Providence?

LESSON

26. *Why do you say that God is a spirit?*

I say that God is a spirit because He has no body, and we cannot see Him or touch Him.

27. *Why do you say that God is eternal?*

I say that God is eternal because He has always existed and He will always exist.

---

[5] Matthew 6:25-32

28. *Why do you say that God is infinitely perfect?*

I say that God is infinitely perfect because He has all perfections, and these perfections are without limit.

• 29. *Why do you say that God is the Creator and Master of all things?*

I say that God is the Creator and Master of all things because He made out of nothing all that exists and everything belongs to Him.

† 30. *What did Jesus Christ ask us to call God?*

Jesus Christ asked us to call God our Father: "Our Father, Who art in heaven…"

• 31. *Is God good, and does He take care of all of His creatures?*

Yes, God is good, and He takes care of all of His creatures; He keeps them in existence and governs them by His Providence.

> NOTE: Providence is God's care for His creatures. Jesus tells us in the Gospel: "The birds of the air neither sow nor harvest, nor do they gather food into barns, and your heavenly Father feeds them. All the more will He take care of you."

† 32. *Where is God?*

God is everywhere: in heaven, on earth and in every place.

† 33. *Does God see everything?*

Yes, God sees everything: the past, the present, the future; all that I do and all that I think.

The Nature and Perfection of God

> **For my life** – I will think of the fact that God is everywhere, that He sees everything, that He knows everything, that I owe Him everything, that He can do everything, and that He loves me, since He created me. I will live in His presence, in confidence and respect.
>
> **Prayer** – Our Father Who art in heaven.
>
> **The Word of God** – "Be you therefore perfect, as also your heavenly Father is perfect." (Matthew 5:28)

Liturgy – People have always built temples to the invisible God. Churches are the houses of God. Love your parish church; discover the beauties of the cathedral in your diocese. We celebrate the anniversary of the consecration of a church; this feast is called its dedication.

Assignment – List everything on earth that proves that God is all-powerful. – What proves that God is good? – Can we hide from God? – What proves that God sees deep inside our heart?

PROJECT – Draw a scene from Bible History which calls to mind the almightiness of God. Draw a scene which calls to mind His goodness.

Lesson 4

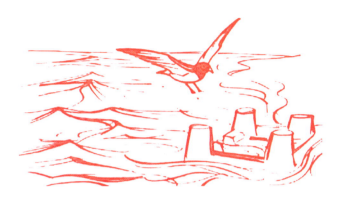

The Mysteries of Religion

If you have ever been to the seaside, you have observed what we call the tide. You did not understand how it could work, so you asked your father or your teacher, and one or the other explained why the water came up and went down with such regularity. Your father and your teacher know things which, for you, are mysteries, that is to say, hidden things.

There are scholars even more intelligent than your father or your teacher, and they teach us what we do not have the time to study or what we do not have the intelligence to understand. Yet even they cannot explain everything. But our good God, Who does know everything, acted as a father for us, or as a teacher, or as a scholar. He taught us truths which we could never have known without Him. These truths tell us about God Himself and what He has done for us; we call them divine mysteries.

Soon you will study the chapters which will teach you that in God there are three Persons: the Father, the Son and the Holy Ghost; that the Son became man and died for us on the Cross. And yet, think about it. When you make the sign of the cross, you are showing that you know these three mysteries.

REVIEW – What have you observed at the seaside? – Who can explain the tide to you? – Why does God know more than all of the scholars put together? – How does God act toward us? – What does the sign of the cross call to your mind?

LESSON _____

- 34. *What is a mystery?*

A mystery is a truth which we must believe because God has made it known to us, but which we cannot perfectly understand.

† 35. *What are the principal mysteries of religion?*

The principal mysteries of religion are: the mystery of the Holy Trinity, the mystery of the Incarnation, and the mystery of the Redemption.

† 36. *What is the sign which reminds you of the principal mysteries of religion?*

The sign which reminds me of the principal mysteries of religion is the sign of the cross.

> NOTE: We should make the sign of the cross morning and night, at the beginning and at the end of our prayers, and also in danger and temptation.

37. *How does the sign of the cross remind us of the unity and the Trinity of God?*

The sign of the cross reminds us of the unity and the Trinity of God because in saying, "In the Name," we affirm that there is only one God; and in saying, "of the Father and of the Son and of the Holy Ghost," we affirm that in God there are three truly distinct Persons.

38. *How does the sign of the cross remind us of the Incarnation and the Redemption?*

The sign of the cross reminds us of the Incarnation, and the Passion and the death of Jesus, because the Son of God made man suffered and died on the Cross.

FOR MY LIFE – I will always make with faith and respect the sign of the cross, which reminds me of the principal mysteries of religion.

PRAYERS – In the Name of the Father and of the Son and of the Holy Ghost.

THE WORD OF GOD – "He that is a searcher of majesty shall be overwhelmed by glory." (Proverbs 25:27)

LITURGY – The Church honors the Cross on which Jesus died, because it is the most expressive symbol and most complete summary of the principal mysteries of religion. There are (two) great feasts of the Cross: (the Finding of the Holy Cross, May 3rd), and the Exaltation of the Holy Cross, September 14th.

The liturgical vestments are red.

ASSIGNMENT – Do you always understand your teacher? – Why do you not always understand him? – Would you understand what a great scholar told you? – Is it surprising that you do not completely understand everything that God has made known? – What is the word for things which God has made known and which you do not understand?

PROJECT – Draw and make a triptych showing three great mysteries (example: the Baptism of Our Lord, the manger, the Crucifixion).

Lesson 5

Mystery of the Holy Trinity

Listen closely to the words of the "I believe in God". You say, "I believe in God, the Father Almighty...; in Jesus Christ His only Son...; in the Holy Ghost..." In this way you are stating that there is only one God, but that in Him there are three Persons.

Who is it that taught us this mystery clearly? It is the Son of God Himself, Our Lord Jesus Christ.

At the beginning of His public life, Jesus came to John the Baptist, who was on the banks of the Jordan, so that John might give Him the baptism of penance. He wanted to show in this way that He was taking on Himself all of the sins of the world. John the Baptist, who knew that Jesus was the Messiah, did not want to baptize Him. Jesus obliged him to do it. Then when Jesus came out of the water, the people heard God the Father saying: "This is My beloved Son, in Whom I am well pleased," and they saw the Holy Ghost appearing above Jesus like a dove floating on the wind.[6] The Holy Trinity manifested Itself in this way.

Before going back up to heaven, after His mission was over, Jesus said to His Apostles: "Going therefore, teach ye all nations: baptizing them in the name of the Father and of the Son and of the Holy Ghost."[7]

REVIEW – What do you affirm when you say the "I believe in God"? – When did Jesus have Himself baptized by John the Baptist? – What happened after Jesus' baptism? – At what other time did Jesus speak of the Holy Trinity?

LESSON

† 39. *What is the mystery of the Holy Trinity?*

The mystery of the Holy Trinity is the mystery of one God in three equal and distinct Persons.

† 40. *Who are the three Persons of the Holy Trinity?*

The three Persons of the Holy Trinity are the Father, the Son, and the Holy Ghost.

41. *Is each one of the three Persons of the Holy Trinity really God?*

Yes, each one of the three Persons of the Holy Trinity is God: the Father is God, the Son is God, and the Holy Ghost is God.

---

[6] Matthew 3:17
[7] Matthew 28:19

42. *Are the Father, the Son and the Holy Ghost really three Gods?*

No, the Father, the Son and the Holy Ghost are not three Gods but one and the same God.

43. *Why are the Father, the Son, and the Holy Ghost one and the same God?*

The Father, the Son, and the Holy Ghost are one and the same God because they have one and the same nature.

> NOTE: Consequently they have the same intelligence, the same will, the same love.

44. *Are the three Divine Persons equal in all things?*

Yes, the three Divine Persons are equal in all things for, being one and the same God, they all Three have the same perfections.

• 45. *Who told us of the mystery of the Holy Trinity?*

It is Jesus Christ who told us of the mystery of the Holy Trinity.

> **FOR MY LIFE** – I will think of the Holy Trinity Who came into my soul at Baptism. If ever I have chased the Trinity away by a serious sin, I will go to Confession as soon as I can.
>
> **PRAYER** – Glory be to the Father, and to the Son, and to the Holy Ghost. As it was in the beginning, is now and ever shall be, world without end. Amen.
>
> **THE WORD OF GOD** – "The grace of Our Lord Jesus Christ and the charity of God and the communication of the Holy Ghost be with you all." (II Cor. 13:13).

LITURGY – On the first Sunday after Pentecost, the Church celebrates the Feast of the Holy Trinity, to honor in a very particular way the great mystery of one God in three Persons.

The liturgical vestments are white.

MYSTERY OF THE HOLY TRINITY

ASSIGNMENT – In whose name were you baptized? – In whose name were your sins forgiven? – Does the priest make many signs of the cross at Mass? – List the ones you have noticed. – Of what mystery does the sign of the cross remind us? – When do we usually make the sign of the cross?

PROJECT – With different colors of tissue paper make stained glass windows representing the various symbols of the Most Holy Trinity.

Lesson 6

Angels and Devils

Right after His baptism, Jesus withdrew into the desert. There he fasted for forty days and forty nights, and then He was hungry. That is when Satan appeared. You know that Satan is one of those angels who rebelled against God and, after being chased out of heaven forever, became a devil. He tried to tempt Jesus. The Gospel tells us in detail about three temptations. At the end of the third, Christ pushed the tempter away by saying to him: "Be gone, Satan..." At that moment angels came down from heaven and served Him.[8]

So there exist both good and bad spirits. The bad ones seek to harm us by presenting sin as something good. The good ones, on the contrary, protect us and

---

[8] Matthew 4:1-11

ANGELS AND DEVILS

help us to obey God. They give us good thoughts and good desires.

You have an angel who guards you and to whom you can pray in temptations and dangers. Be faithful in following his inspirations.

REVIEW – What did Jesus do after His baptism? – Who appeared before Him? – Could Jesus have sinned? – Who came to serve Jesus? – Do the bad angels pay any attention to us? – Do the good angels?

LESSON

† 46. *Which are the most perfect creatures?*

The most perfect creatures are angels and men.

† 47. *What are angels?*

Angels are spirits whom God created to adore and to serve Him.

48. *In what state did God create the angels?*

God created the angels happy and good.

• 49. *Did all of the angels remain good?*

No, all of the angels did not remain good; a large number rebelled against God.

50. *What do we call the angels who rebelled against God?*

The angels who rebelled against God are called devils.

† 51. *What do the good angels do for us?*

The good angels protect us and encourage us to do good. Each one of us has a guardian angel.

• 52. *What do the devils do against us?*

The devils seek to hurt us and to lead us into sin by temptation.

• 53. *Can you resist the devils?*

Yes, I can resist the devils with the help of God, which I obtain through prayer.

> **NOTE: Jesus said, "Watch ye: and pray that ye enter not into temptation." (Matthew 26:41)**

FOR MY LIFE – In danger and temptation, I will remember to call upon my guardian angel to help me.

PRAYER – Holy guardian angels, watch over us. Preserve us from all evil and from all sin, and do not allow us to give in to temptation.

THE WORD OF GOD – "The Lord hath given His angels charge over thee, to keep thee in all thy ways." (Psalm 90:11)

LITURGY – The Church celebrates the feasts of Saint Michael the Archangel (on May 8th) and September 29th; the Angel Gabriel on March 24th; and the Archangel Raphael on October 24th.

On October 2nd She celebrates the Feast of the Holy Guardian Angels.

The vestments of the priest are white or gold.

ANGELS AND DEVILS

ASSIGNMENT – Have angels often appeared on earth? – In what form do they appear? – Give the names of the angels you know. – To whom have angels appeared?

PROJECT – Find a beautiful picture of a guardian angel and frame it, and then place the picture at the head of your bed.

Lesson 7

The Creation of Man

At the end of the sixth day, God created man in His image and likeness. He formed his body from the slime of the earth and placed in that body a spiritual, immortal soul, capable of knowing and loving his Creator. God named the first man Adam. He then sent Adam into a deep sleep and from his flesh He formed the body of the first woman, Eve. Man therefore has a body and a soul. Do you want to know the value of the soul? Read carefully what follows.

One day as Jesus was teaching, He made this statement: "Fear ye not them that kill the body, and are not able to kill the soul, but rather fear Him that can destroy both body and soul in hell." Jesus thereby showed that what counts in man is his soul.

The soul is in fact a spirit created in the image of God; it is the soul that thinks, that wills, that loves. The body is only the servant or the instrument of the spirit. When you reflect, and when you study at school, you are using your soul.

THE CREATION OF MAN

Your body will fall into dust after your death but your soul will continue to live; it cannot die. The reason you are learning your catechism well is to prepare for this life that will never end.

REVIEW – How did God form the body of the first man? – What did He name the first man? the first woman? – What is it in man that makes him resemble God? – What words did Jesus use to show the value of the soul? – What can you do with your soul?

LESSON

† 54. *What is man?*

Man is a rational creature composed of a body and a soul.

† 55. *What is the soul?*

The soul is an immortal spirit which God created in His likeness to be united to a body.

56. *How do you know that you have a soul?*

I know that I have a soul because without a soul I could neither think, nor reflect, nor will freely.

> NOTE: You do not possess anything more precious than your soul. Jesus said: "What doth it profit a man, if he gain the whole world and suffer the loss of his own soul?" (Matthew 16:26)

† 57. *Why did God create us?*

God created us to know Him, to love Him and to serve Him as our Father, and so to gain happiness in heaven.

† 58. *Who was the first man and who was the first woman?*

The first man was Adam and the first woman was Eve; they are our first parents.

> FOR MY LIFE – God created me in His image and likeness. I will try hard not to destroy what the good God has made, by committing a sin.
>
> PRAYER – Lord, I am the work of Your almighty power and of Your love which drew me out of nothingness. I thank You and I adore You.
>
> THE WORD OF GOD – In the beginning, God made man in His image and likeness. (Genesis 1:26.)

Who discovered it
Who maintains it
Why Him alone **?**

LITURGY – Lent is the fast of forty days which the Church has established in memory of the fast of Our

Lord Jesus Christ in the desert, to prepare us by penance for the feast of Easter.

Lent begins on Ash Wednesday. On that day, the celebrant imposes ashes on the foreheads of the faithful, saying: "Remember, man, that thou art dust, and unto dust thou shalt return." These words remind us that God formed man from the slime of the earth.

The liturgical color of Ash Wednesday is violet.

ASSIGNMENT – What makes man resemble God? – In what way is man different from God? – In what way is man different from an animal?

PROJECT – Design a leaflet whose different pages represent the successive creations of God.

Lesson 8

Original Sin

Have you ever felt within yourself something pushing you to do evil? For example you promise to be calm, and then you become angry over nothing; you decide to work hard and suddenly you give in to your laziness... The reason is that you have inside of you an inclination to evil which comes from the sin committed by our first parents, Adam and Eve.

God had created them intelligent and good. They were happy in the earthly Paradise; they did not know what pain was; they were never to die.

In their soul they possessed grace, that is to say, the very life of God. The Creator loved them, looked on them as His children, and prepared for them the eternal joys of His heaven.

So they were like children who receive everything from their father, and who are to inherit his entire fortune. Yet they were free to continue living in the friendship of God or to separate themselves from Him.

Then came the test. There was a tree in the earthly Paradise called the tree of the knowledge of good and evil. God had forbidden them to eat of its fruit. "If you eat of its fruit, you will die," He had told them. Now, the devil one day said to Eve: "Eat of that fruit and you shall be as gods, knowing good and evil." Alas! Eve listened to the tempter; and not only did she eat of the fruit but she gave some of it to Adam, who also ate of it. Thus they separated themselves from their heavenly Father in order to follow the rebellious angel.

They had lost the friendship of God and the right to inherit heaven; they felt themselves inclined toward evil; they began to suffer, and one day they would die.

Worse yet, since they had willfully destroyed their riches which were the friendship of God and happiness for their soul and their body, they could not pass them on to their descendants. This is the reason why, when you are born, you are deprived of the grace of God and have no right to the happiness of heaven; this is the reason why you feel in your soul an inclination to do evil and why you suffer in your body; this is the reason why you will die, for all men have this original sin. The only one ever preserved from it is the Most Blessed Virgin Mary, the Mother of Jesus the Savior, whose story you will soon learn.

You will also see how Jesus gave us back the friendship of God.

REVIEW – Do you always do the good you want to do? – To whom can you compare Adam and Eve in the earthly

Paradise? – What had God forbidden them to do? – Who sought to make them disobey? – What happened? – Why are you inclined toward evil?

LESSON _____

† 59. *In what state did God create Adam and Eve?*

God created Adam and Eve happy and holy.

• 60. *How many kinds of life did God give to Adam and Eve?*

God gave two kinds of life to Adam and Eve:
  1. Natural life, uniting their soul to their body;
  2. Supernatural life, uniting their soul to the three Divine Persons.

61. *Did Adam and Eve receive any extraordinary gifts from God?*

Yes, Adam and Eve received certain extraordinary gifts from God: they were not attracted by sin, and they would neither suffer nor die.

> NOTE: Adam and Eve also possessed a very vast knowledge.

62. *On what condition could Adam and Eve remain holy and happy?*

Adam and Eve could remain holy and happy on the condition that they obey God.

63. *Did Adam and Eve remain subject to God?*

No, Adam and Eve did not remain subject to God but disobeyed, deceived by the devil.

64. *What did Adam and Eve lose by disobeying God?*

By disobeying God, Adam and Eve lost the life which was to lead them to heaven; they were condemned to suffering and death, and from then on felt themselves attracted to sin.

65. *Is the sin of Adam passed on to all of his descendants?*

Yes, the sin of Adam is passed on to all of his descendants, who are all born deprived of grace and subject to the same miseries as he.

66. *What is the name of the state in which all men since Adam are born?*

The state in which all men since Adam are born is called Original Sin.

67. *Was the Blessed Virgin preserved from Original Sin?*

Yes, the Blessed Virgin was preserved from Original Sin. For this reason we say that she was conceived without sin.

> NOTE: We celebrate this privilege of the Blessed Virgin on the Feast of the Immaculate Conception, December 8th.

> **FOR MY LIFE** – I will think about the fact that sin is the greatest of all evils because it makes us lose Paradise, the greatest of all goods.
>
> **PRAYER** – Lead us not into temptation, but deliver us from evil.
>
> **THE WORD OF GOD** – "Wherefore as by one man sin entered into this world and by sin death: and so death passed upon all men." (Rom. 5:12)

LITURGY – On December 8th, the Church celebrates the Feast of the Immaculate Conception to honor the privilege by which the Most Blessed Virgin was preserved from Original Sin.

The liturgical color is white or gold.

ASSIGNMENT – Make two columns. Write in one all that Adam and Eve possessed before the Fall. In the other, write all that they possessed after the Fall.

PROJECT – Frame a picture of Our Lady of Lourdes with the words around it that the Blessed Virgin spoke to Bernadette: "I am the Immaculate Conception."

THE HISTORY OF SALVATION

We call "History of Salvation", the account of everything God did to give back to men His friendship and the happiness lost by sin.

We can divide this History into three parts:

1. **GOD PREPARES THE COMING OF THE SAVIOR**: The first Patriarchs, from Adam to Noah, kept faith in the true God and hoped in His promise. Then God chose a people with whom He made an alliance (the Old Covenant or the Old Testament).
2. **GOD SENDS THE SAVIOR**: By His life and His sacrifice, the Savior establishes the "New Covenant" of God with men (the New Testament) and founds the new People of God, the Church.
3. **THE SAVIOR CONTINUES HIS WORK THROUGH THE CHURCH**: By Her, God saves men until the end of the world.

The "History of Salvation" will last until the end of the world; the Kingdom of God will then be established in all its perfection.

SUMMARY OF THE "HISTORY OF SALVATION"

1ST PART: GOD PREPARES THE COMING OF THE SAVIOR

God decides to save humanity

In creating the world, God willed the happiness of man. Man became unhappy by his own fault. He did not want to submit to the will of God.

The Love of God did not abandon men. By a marvelous disposition of His infinite wisdom, He willed to draw good out of evil. He decided to send His only Son Who would bring creation back to its Master. The Son of God would become man, and would save us by dying on the Cross.

Distant preparations

Immediately after the first sin, God promised Adam and Eve that He would send a Savior. He asked men to adore Him alone and to trust in His promise.

Noah and the Flood

As the centuries passed, the descendants of Adam and Eve multiplied upon the earth. Some of them remained faithful to God, such as Abel and Noah. Most forgot about God and fell into idolatry. They lived in sin. Cain killed his brother. The misbehavior of humanity deserved its total destruction. Yet in the midst of the greatest cataclysms, God had pity on humanity. After the Flood He "made a covenant" with Noah, who had remained faithful to Him.

The descendants of Noah fell again into evil; out of pride they offended God and built the Tower of Babel.

Around 1800 years before the coming of the Savior

God then chose Abraham to make of him the leader of a chosen people. He asked him to leave his country; He "made a covenant" with him, and promised him that he would be the father of a numerous people from whom would be born the Savior of the world.

The Patriarchs

The descendants of Abraham became the leaders of the twelve tribes who formed the People of Israel.

During a famine, the Israelites moved to Egypt; they remained there for around 400 years, first happily, then reduced to slavery.

Moses 1250

Moses was chosen by God to be the liberator and the leader of the chosen people. The Israelites left Egypt and, after crossing the Red Sea, entered into the desert, where God led them and miraculously fed them. The Jews celebrated the anniversary of this deliverance every year, at the Feast of the Passover.

On Mount Sinai, God gave them the Commandments and renewed the covenant made with Abraham. Moses gathered the Israelite tribes into one nation, gave them laws, and organized the divine worship. For forty years he led them through the desert toward the Promised Land.

The Judges

Under the guidance of Joshua, the Israelites entered into the Promised Land (Palestine) and settled there little by little. Several times God raised up judges to direct and protect them. Samuel, the last judge, established Saul as king of Israel.

The Kings 1000

Saul was succeeded by David, the great prophet-king. He regrouped and reorganized the People of God; he chose Jerusalem as the capital and the religious center of the people of Israel. Solomon, his son, succeeded him; he constructed the Temple and organized the divine worship.

The Prophets

At the death of Solomon, the kingdom divided into two: the Kingdom of Judah (whose capital was Jerusalem) and the Kingdom of Israel (whose capital was Samaria). Their kings were sometimes faithful, but very often unfaithful to the Covenant with God. God sent them prophets, of whom the greatest were Isaiah, Elias and Eliseus.

Exile 721

The Assyrians captured the kingdom of Israel; they led part of the nation into exile and put an end to the kingdom of Israel.

587

The kingdom of Judah survived for around 150 more years; it fell back into impiety, in spite of the warnings of the prophet Jeremiah. It was attacked by Nabuchodonosor, king of Babylon; Jerusalem was taken and burned, the Temple was destroyed, and the people led into captivity in Babylon.

In Babylon, the prophets Ezechiel and Daniel maintained the faith and the hope of the Israelites, and reminded them of the divine promises.

The Jewish people 536

Babylon was taken by Cyrus, king of Persia, who authorized the Israelites to return to their homeland. They rebuilt the Temple and reorganized the divine worship. Under the direction of Esdras and Nehemiah, they renewed the Covenant with God. After all of their hardships, they understood better how much they needed the Savior promised by God.

333

Following the conquests of Alexander the Great, the country fell under the domination of the Greeks for 200 years.

143

The persecutions of Antiochus sparked a national and religious uprising directed by the Maccabees, and the Jews were free again for 80 years.

As a result of Jewish infighting, the Romans came to occupy the country. Palestine was made part of a Roman province.

The Savior was about to come.

2ND PART: GOD SENDS THE SAVIOR

The Savior

Jesus Christ, the Son of God made man, was born at Bethlehem. At the age of 30 years, He traveled throughout Palestine announcing that He was the promised Savior. He taught the Good News of the Kingdom of God.

This Kingdom is not an earthly kingdom; it is the kingdom of all those who believe in Jesus Christ and become the children of God.

The New People of God

The new People of God would no longer be limited to one nation; all men of all countries are called to be a part of it.

The leaders of the Jewish people were opposed to the message of the Savior; Jesus was arrested and condemned to death. He offered His sufferings and

death to God as a sacrifice for the sins of men; thus He established forever the New Covenant of God with men.

He resurrected glorious, showing that He is the conqueror of death and sin.

He confided to the Apostles the mission of continuing His work and He promised them the Holy Ghost; then He ascended gloriously into heaven.

3RD PART: THE SAVIOR CONTINUES HIS WORK THROUGH THE CHURCH

The Church

After Pentecost, the Apostles, filled with the Holy Ghost, preached the Gospel and organized the Church of Jesus Christ.

From then on, the Christian People, the Church of Jesus Christ, became the veritable People of God, heir to the promises of the divine Covenants.

Through the Church, the Savior continues to announce to men the Good News of Salvation; He brings

them the life of grace and leads them toward the happiness of heaven.

"The History of Salvation" will last until the end of the world, when the Savior will return visibly in order to judge all men; the Kingdom of God will then have attained its full perfection.

The Savior Promised and Given to the World Is the Son of God Made Man.

HIS NAME IS JESUS CHRIST.

"And the Word was made flesh and dwelt among us." (John 1:24)

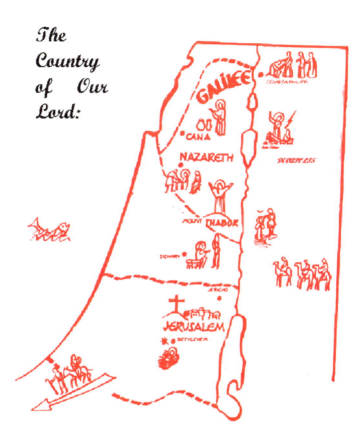

SURFACE AREA: around 11,000 square miles
BORDERS: to the north, Syria and Phoenicia; to the south, Idumea and the deserts touching Egypt; to the east, the region of Arabia and Ituraea; to the west, the Mediterranean.
RIVER: the Jordan, which flows into the Dead Sea.
LAKES: Lake Merom; the great lake of Tiberias.
PROVINCES: west of the Jordan: Galilee, Samaria, Judea; and east of the Jordan, the Decapolis and Peraea.
CLIMATE: rather harsh winters; very hot summers with cool nights. The soil produces fruits in abundance: figs, nuts, apples, oranges, pomegranates, etc.
TREES: palm trees, tamarisks, cypresses, terebinths, etc.

Lesson 9

Second and Third Articles of the Creed

"...And in Jesus Christ, His only Son, Our Lord, Who was conceived of the Holy Ghost, was born of the Virgin Mary..."

The Mystery of the Incarnation

I. Our Lord Jesus Christ

God had promised Adam and Eve that He would give them a Savior. Long after the Fall, He chose for Himself a small nation to whom He gave the country which we now call Palestine. Everything that happened to this nation is told in the "History of Salvation." We read that God renewed the promise of the Savior to Abraham, to the patriarchs Isaac and Jacob, and finally to the prophets, who kept the Jewish people from forgetting the true God and who announced the coming of the Messiah. He came at the appointed time.

The awaited Messiah is Jesus. Jesus is the Son of God made man. He has a body and a soul like ours. His mother is the Blessed Virgin Mary. He is named Jesus, which means Savior.

But He is not only a man; He is God, the Son of God, the second Person of the Holy Trinity. When Jesus says: "I am hungry, I am thirsty, I suffer," or when He says to a sick person: "I will it, be healed," He is speaking as a man and He is speaking as God, but it is always the Person of the Son of God who speaks; there is in Him only one Person.

This mystery of the Son of God Who becomes man is the mystery of the Incarnation.

REVIEW – To whom did God promise a Savior? – What country did God give to the Jewish people? – Where is the history of this people told? – Is Jesus a man? – Is He God? – How many persons are there in Him?

LESSON

- 68. *Did God abandon men after the sin of Adam and Eve?*

No, God did not abandon men after the sin of Adam and Eve, but He promised them a Savior.

69. *Did the promised Savior come?*

Yes, the promised Savior came; He is the Son of God made man.

The Mystery of the Incarnation

† 70. *What is the mystery of the Incarnation?*

The mystery of the Incarnation is the mystery of the Son of God made man.

† 71. *How did the Son of God become man?*

The Son of God became man by taking a body and a soul like ours in the womb of the Blessed Virgin Mary.

72. *Why did the Son of God become man?*

The Son of God became man to save us, and to teach us by His word and His example.

† 73. *What is the name of the Son of God made man?*

The Son of God made man is named Jesus Christ.

> NOTE: The name "Jesus" means Savior, that is to say, redeemer and priest.
>
> We also call Jesus "Our Lord," that is, Our Master, because He created us and is king of all men.

• 74. *Is Jesus Christ truly God?*

Yes, Jesus Christ is truly God, because He is the Son of God, equal to His Father in all things.

> NOTE: "For God so loved the world, as to give His only begotten Son." (John 3:16)

• 75. *Is Jesus Christ truly man?*

Yes, Jesus Christ is truly man because He has a body and a soul as we do.

76. *How many natures are there in Jesus Christ?*

There are two natures in Jesus Christ: the divine nature because He is God, and a human nature because He is man.

77. *How many persons are there in Jesus Christ?*

There is only one person in Jesus Christ, the Person of the Son of God.

> FOR MY LIFE – I will think about the fact that the tiny baby in the manger is nevertheless He "by whom all things were made," and I will adore Him.
>
> PRAYER – My Lord and My God!
>
> THE WORD OF GOD – "The Word was made flesh." (John 1:14)

LITURGY – To prepare us to celebrate properly the Feast of Christmas, the Church has instituted the season of Advent which is made up of the four Sundays preceding Christmas. It is a time of prayer and penance. The priest wears purple vestments at the altar and we do not sing the "Gloria in Excelsis" (at Sunday and ferial Masses).

On March 25th, the Feast of the Annunciation, the priest wears white or gold vestments.

ASSIGNMENT – Look for proofs in the life of Jesus which confirm that He is a man like us, and then look for proofs which show that He is God.

PROJECT – Draw two pictures, one showing that Jesus is God, the other showing that Jesus is man.

Lesson 10

The Mystery of the Incarnation (Continued)

II: The Most Blessed Virgin Mary

Nazareth was a little town of about 3,000 inhabitants. It was located on high ground, and from far away one sees its white houses built all along and up the sides of the hill. From the highest part of the town one can make out the rich fields of Galilee covered in flowers, vineyards, and shade trees.

In one of the humblest houses, a young girl named Mary, descendant of the royal family of David, was deep in prayer. All at once the Angel Gabriel appeared to her and said: "Hail, Mary, full of grace, the Lord is with thee; blessed art thou among women." Since the Virgin was troubled at these words, the angel added: "Fear not, Mary, for thou has found grace with God. Behold thou shalt...bring forth a son: and thou shalt call His name Jesus. He shall be great and shall be called the Son of the Most High. And the Lord God shall give unto Him the throne of

David His father....And of His kingdom there shall be no end." Then Mary answered: "How shall this be done?" The angel replied: "The Holy Ghost shall come upon thee and the power of the Most High shall overshadow thee. And therefore also the Holy which shall be born of thee shall be called the Son of God." Mary, bowing her head, accepted to be the mother of the Son of God by saying: "Behold the handmaid of the Lord: be it done to me according to thy word."[9]

Now, Mary was engaged to be married to a just man, Joseph the carpenter, who in turn accepted to be the spouse of the Virgin and the foster father of Jesus.

REVIEW – What do you know about Nazareth? – Which angel appeared to the Virgin? – What did he say to her? – With what words did the Virgin accept to be the mother of Jesus? – What do you know about Joseph?

LESSON

• 78. *Who announced to the Blessed Virgin that she would be the Mother of Jesus Christ?*

It was the Angel Gabriel who announced to the Blessed Virgin that she would be the Mother of Jesus Christ. The Church reminds us of this event on March 25th, the Feast of the Annunciation.

---

[9] Luke 1:26-38

THE MYSTERY OF THE INCARNATION (CONTINUED)

† 79. *Should the Blessed Virgin Mary be called the Mother of God?*

Yes, the Blessed Virgin Mary should be called the Mother of God because she is the Mother of a Son Who is God.

• 80. *Is the Blessed Virgin Mary our Mother also?*

Yes, the Blessed Virgin Mary is our Mother also, and on the cross Jesus said to Saint John who represented us: "Behold your mother."

• 81. *Who was Saint Joseph?*

Saint Joseph was the spouse of the Virgin Mary, the foster father of Jesus, and the head of the Holy Family.

FOR MY LIFE – When the Angelus rings, I will think about the great event it reminds us of, and I will repeat the salutation of the Angel Gabriel, to the glory of the Most Blessed Virgin.

PRAYER – "Hail, Mary..."

THE WORD OF GOD – Mary answered the Angel Gabriel: "Behold the handmaid of the Lord: be it done unto me according to thy word." (Luke 1:38)

SINCE YOU ARE OUR MOTHER

Our Lady, all of your children
Come to say their prayers with you,
Since you are our mother.

If sometimes we are bad,
Oh! do not be too angry,
Since you are our mother.

Make us more obedient,
Turn us into true apostles,
Since you are our mother.

May Jesus always have the first place
In our hearts of children,
Since you are our mother.

—Jean Servel

LITURGY

1. There are many feasts in honor of the Blessed Virgin. The most solemn is that of the Assumption which is celebrated on August 15th. This feast reminds us that Mary, raised from the dead, was lifted body and soul into heaven, where she is above the angels and the saints. It is one of the six holy days of obligation (in the United States).

The priest wears white or gold vestments. 2. On March 19th, the Church celebrates the Feast of St. Joseph, as spouse of the Most Blessed Virgin; and,

The Mystery of the Incarnation (continued)

after Easter (May 1st), as patron of the universal Church.

ASSIGNMENT – What are the principal shrines in honor of the Most Blessed Virgin in your diocese?

PROJECT – Design a frieze of the different apparitions of the Blessed Virgin. Build a grotto of Lourdes.

LESSON 11

THE CHILDHOOD AND THE YOUTH OF OUR LORD JESUS CHRIST

Mary and Joseph lived in Nazareth. However, the prophet Micheas had foretold that the Savior would be born in Bethlehem. That is what happened. The Roman emperor wanted to know the number of his subjects, and he ordered everyone to register in his home country. For Mary and Joseph, that was Bethlehem.

Look on the map: from Nazareth to Bethlehem is a journey of more than seventy miles.

They arrived in that town in the evening, tired after their long journey: but finding no place for them at the inn, they turned toward the countryside. They saw a sort of cave which was used as a stable and they entered there to rest. At midnight, Jesus, the Son of God, the Son of the Virgin Mary, came into the world. The Virgin wrapped the Child in swaddling clothes and laid him in a manger, that is to say, in a feeding trough for animals.

Now there were shepherds in the surrounding area, keeping watch over their flocks. All of a sudden they were surrounded by a great light; an angel appeared to them and said: "Fear not; for, behold, I bring you good tidings of great joy that shall be to all the people: for, this day is born to you a Savior, Who is Christ the Lord, in the city of David. And this shall be a sign unto you. You shall find the infant wrapped in swaddling clothes and laid in a manger."

At the same moment, many other angels joined the first one and they all said: "Glory to God in the highest: and on earth peace to men of good will."

When the angels had left them, the shepherds said to one another: "Let us go over to Bethlehem and let us see this word that is come to pass, which the Lord hath made known to us." They soon discovered the grotto, entered in, and adored the Infant Jesus.

If you want to know what happened to the Infant Jesus after His birth, read carefully the answers to the lesson and listen to the explanations that will be given to you. You should know very well the life of Him Who is our good Master.

REVIEW – What had the prophet Micheas announced? – Why did Mary and Joseph go to Bethlehem? – How did people travel long ago? – Why did Joseph and Mary take refuge in a cave? – What happened at midnight? – How were the shepherds told? – What did they do?

LESSON _____

82. *Where is the life of Jesus Christ told?*

The life of Jesus Christ is told in the four Gospels written by Saint Matthew, Saint Mark, Saint Luke, and Saint John.

† 83. *Where was Jesus Christ born?*

Jesus Christ was born in Bethlehem, a little town of Judea, in a poor stable.

• 84. *On what day do we celebrate the birth of Jesus Christ?*

We celebrate the birth of Jesus Christ on December 25th, Christmas Day.

85. *To whom was the birth of Jesus Christ first announced?*

The birth of Jesus Christ was first announced to shepherds by angels, and then to Magi by a miraculous star.

86. *On what day did Our Lord receive the name of Jesus?*

Our Lord received the name of Jesus on the eighth day after His birth.

87. *When was Jesus Christ presented to God in the Temple?*

Jesus Christ was presented to God in the Temple forty days after His birth.

NOTE: The Church celebrates this feast on February 2nd. The Presentation in the Temple is also called the "Purification of the Blessed Virgin."

88. *Where was the Infant Jesus brought shortly after His birth?*

Shortly after His birth, the Infant Jesus was brought into Egypt to escape the anger of Herod, who wanted to kill Him.

NOTE: The Holy Family returned to Nazareth after the death of Herod. It is there that Jesus lived until He was thirty years old.

† 89. *What was the life of Jesus at Nazareth?*

The life of Jesus at Nazareth was a life of prayer, obedience and work.

NOTE: The Gospel teaches us that, at Nazareth, Jesus was subject to His parents, and that He grew in age and wisdom before God and before men.

90. *What did Jesus do when He was twelve years old?*

When Jesus was twelve years old He went with His parents to the Temple in Jerusalem, where He astonished the Doctors of the Law by the wisdom of His answers.

> **FOR MY LIFE** – I will try to imitate Jesus in His hidden life, especially His humility, His work and His obedience.
>
> **PRAYER** – "Glory to God in the highest."
>
> **THE WORD OF GOD** – "God so loved the world, as to give His only begotten Son: that whoever believeth in Him may not perish, but may have life everlasting." (John 3:16)

LITURGY – On December 25th the Church celebrates the Feast of Christmas, or the feast of the birth of Jesus Christ. On that day, priests may celebrate three Masses: Midnight Mass, Mass at dawn, and the Mass of the day. The priest wears white or gold vestments. Christmas is one of the six holy days of obligation (in the United States).

ASSIGNMENT – What are the principal events of the life of Jesus which were foretold by the prophets? – What prophets do you know about? – What is the season of the year which recalls the time during which men awaited the Savior? – What do you know about Saint John the Baptist?

PROJECT – Make a map of Palestine and draw in red the distance traveled by the Holy Family until their return to Nazareth. Make a nativity scene representing as well as possible the manger at Bethlehem.

Lesson 12

The Public Life of Our Lord

Do you like books? Then ask to be given the most beautiful book of all: the Gospels.

They were written by two Apostles, Saint Matthew and Saint John, and by two disciples of the Apostles, Saint Mark and Saint Luke.

You can read passages from them in your missal.

Jesus was about thirty years old and was going to begin His public life, that is to say, to show Himself as the Messiah or the Savior of men.

At that time, Saint John the Baptist was preaching penance on the banks of the Jordan, and saying that the Messiah was about to make Himself known.

Jesus went toward him and asked him for Baptism. You know what happened; you were told the story in the chapter on the mystery of the Holy Trinity. Jesus then withdrew into the desert where He fasted for forty days, and was tempted by the devil.

After choosing His Apostles, Jesus began to teach that God is a Father to us, infinitely good and infinitely merciful.

He reminded men that they are all brothers, and that they should love one another as members of a family.

When He spoke about Himself, He said that He was the Son of God.

To be certain that the people understood, He presented His doctrine through beautiful stories, using comparisons called parables.

Those who heard Him were in admiration and said: "Never has a man spoken like this man."

REVIEW – About how old was Jesus when He began His public life? – In what chapter of the catechism do you learn of the baptism of Our Lord? – Where did Jesus withdraw after His baptism? – By whom were the Gospels written? – When did Jesus choose His Apostles? – What did Jesus teach? – How did He teach?

LESSON

• 91. *What did Jesus Christ do when He was about thirty years old?*

When He was about thirty years old, Jesus Christ received the baptism of penance given by Saint John the Baptist on the banks of the Jordan.

> NOTE: The baptism given by Saint John the Baptist was not the sacrament of Baptism, but prepared for the forgiveness of sins by arousing contrition.

The Public Life of Our Lord

- 92. *What did Jesus Christ do after His baptism?*

After His baptism Jesus Christ fasted for forty days in the desert; then He chose His twelve Apostles and began to preach the Gospel.

93. *What does the word "Gospel" mean?*

The word "Gospel" means good news.

94. *What good news did Jesus Christ announce?*

Jesus Christ announced that God is an infinitely good and merciful Father, and that we should love Him with all our heart, always doing His will.

95. *What else did Our Lord teach?*

Our Lord also taught that we are all brothers and that we should love one another.

> NOTE: Jesus said: "All that you wish men to do to you, do unto them."

96. *What did Our Lord say in speaking of Himself?*

In speaking of Himself, Our Lord said that He was the Son of God, the Savior of all men, promised and awaited since the sin of Adam.

97. *How did Jesus speak in order to be better understood by His Apostles?*

In order to be better understood by His Apostles, Jesus used stories, speaking in comparisons called parables.

NOTE: Jesus taught everywhere, in houses, in the synagogues where the Jews gathered to pray, in towns, in villages, and on the shores of the lake.

He especially loved to speak to the poor and the humble.

Those who heard Him were in admiration and said: "Never has a man spoken like this man."

> **FOR MY LIFE** – Lord Jesus, may I receive this good news that You have brought to me, and may I fulfill Your commands.
>
> **PRAYER** – "Thy will be done on earth as it is in heaven."
>
> **THE WORD OF GOD** – "My meat is to do the will of Him that sent Me." (John 4:34)

LITURGY – You will notice that the priest at Mass respectfully kisses the book after the reading of the Gospel.

ASSIGNMENT – What parables do you know?

PROJECT – Illustrate the parable of the sower.

Lesson 13

Our Lord Jesus Christ is God

Jesus Christ proved that He is God by His miracles and by His prophecies

Jesus is God. He was indeed the One foretold by the prophets. He knew the future, and He said how He would die. He foretold that He would rise again, that Jerusalem would be destroyed, and that His Church would last forever. He performed miracles to show that He was God.

One day, while Jesus was speaking, a man named Jairus, being greatly moved, drew near and said to him, "Lord, come quickly to my home, my daughter is dying, come and heal her." His daughter was around twelve years old. While he was speaking to Jesus, someone came to tell him: "Thy daughter is dead: trouble Him not." Jesus said to the poor, sad father: "Fear not. Believe only: and she shall be safe."

When they arrived at the house, they found it full of people making a great deal of noise, weeping, crying out in long moans; and there were even some people playing the flute, according to the custom. Jesus then said: "The maid is not dead." Everyone mocked Him. Jesus made them leave and, going into the room with the father and the mother of the child, He took the hand of the little girl and said to her: "Maid, arise." At that moment, the little dead girl sat up, full of life.[10]

You can read in the Gospel about the resurrection of the widow's son at Naim, and that of Lazarus. You know the greatest of all Christ's miracles: His own resurrection.

Then say to Jesus, like the Apostle Saint Peter: "Jesus, Thou art Christ, the Son of the living God."[11]

REVIEW – What does the Gospel prove? – How do you know that Jesus Christ knew the future? – Tell the miracle of the daughter of Jairus. – What does this miracle prove?

LESSON

• 98. *How do we know that Jesus Christ is God?*
We know that Jesus Christ is God because He clearly affirmed it and because He proved it.

† 99. *How did Jesus Christ prove that He is God?*
Jesus Christ proved that He is God by fulfilling the prophecies and working many miracles.

---

[10] Luke 8:41-56
[11] Matthew 16:16

100. *What is a prophecy?*

A prophecy is the announcement of future events which God alone could know in advance.

101. *Did Jesus Christ make many prophecies?*

Yes, Jesus Christ made many prophecies: He foretold His Passion, His death, His resurrection, the destruction of Jerusalem, and the trials and the triumph of His Church.

102. *What is a miracle?*

A miracle is an extraordinary deed which can only be worked by the power of God.

• 103. *Did Jesus Christ work many miracles?*

Yes, Jesus Christ worked many miracles: He multiplied bread, calmed the storm, cast out devils, healed the sick, and raised the dead.

104. *What was the greatest miracle of Jesus Christ?*

The greatest miracle of Jesus Christ was to raise Himself from the dead. It is the greatest proof that He is God.

105. *How do these prophecies and miracles prove that Jesus Christ is God?*

These prophecies and miracles prove that Jesus Christ is God because He worked them by His own power and because God alone can work them.

> **For my life** – It is because Jesus is the Son of God that He was able to save us. Salvation is in none other. I shall expect it from Him alone.
>
> **Prayer** – "Thou art Christ, the Son of the living God."
>
> **The Word of God** – "In the name of Jesus, every knee should bow, of those that are in heaven, on earth, and under the earth." (Philip. 2:10)

Liturgy – In your missal, find the Gospels of the Third and Fourth Sundays after Epiphany, which tell the story of the miracles worked by Our Lord over illness and over nature. The Third Sunday of Lent tells the story of a miracle over a devil, and the Fifth Sunday after Pentecost tells the story of a miracle over death.

Assignment – Use three columns to list the miracles Jesus worked:

Miracles over things	Healing	Raising from the dead

Project – Build a small stage with movable characters or a diorama representing the miracle of Our Lord which struck you the most.

LESSON 14

FOURTH AND FIFTH ARTICLES OF THE CREED

"He suffered under Pontius Pilate, was crucified, died, and was buried. He descended into hell..."

THE MYSTERY OF THE REDEMPTION

When you see a crucifix, or when you recite the words of the "I believe in God": "He suffered under Pontius Pilate, was crucified, died," think of everything that Jesus endured for our sins.

On Holy Thursday evening, after the meal at which He had given the Eucharist, Jesus withdrew into the Garden of Olives. There He could see all the sins of the world, and He offered His life to His Father in order to take them away.

Jesus was praying alone, when a band of Jews, guided by the traitor Judas, came to arrest Him. He allowed Himself to be captured. Seeing Him surrounded by enemies, the Apostles all fled.

The Mystery of the Redemption

Jesus was brought before the tribunal of the Jews presided by the high priest Caiphas, who condemned Him to death. For the rest of the night, He remained with the soldiers and the servants of the Temple. These men beat Him and then put a blindfold over His eyes and each one in turn came before Him, slapped His face, and said: "Tell us who hit You."

But the death sentence had to be confirmed by the governor, Pontius Pilate. The governor understood the injustice committed and sought to deliver Christ. Learning that Jesus was from Galilee, he sent Him to Herod, who was at the head of that province and who happened to be in Jerusalem on that day. But Herod only mocked Him and sent Him back to Pilate.

Pilate tried again to let Jesus go. In the end, he was too afraid of the people and condemned Jesus to death, after ordering Him to be scourged heavily with whips and leather straps.

At last Jesus was brought to Calvary. He had climbed to the top, weighed down by the cross. They removed His clothes. They made Him stretch out on the wood, and they nailed Him to it through His hands and through His feet. They crucified two thieves beside Him. It was around noon.

The cross was settled into the ground. Jesus looked at His executioners and He said to God: "Father, forgive them, for they know not what they do."

One of the criminals who was dying with Him repented, and Jesus said to him: "This day thou shalt be with Me in Paradise."

The Virgin Mary and Saint John were standing at the foot of the cross. Then Jesus, turning His eyes toward Saint John, said to Mary: "Behold thy son," and to Saint John: "Behold thy mother."

But Jesus crucified was suffering from a terrible thirst and He cried out: "I thirst." One of the soldiers used a sponge fastened to the end of a stick to moisten the lips of the condemned Man with a mixture of water and vinegar. "It is consummated," said Jesus, and then addressing Himself to His Father: "Father, into Thy hands I commend My spirit." He was dead. It was then around three o'clock in the afternoon.

To be certain that He was dead, one of the soldiers pierced His heart with a lance.

REVIEW – What happened in the Garden of Olives? – Who betrayed Jesus? – Where was Jesus led? – What did Pontius Pilate want? – Why did he condemn Jesus? – Among the words spoken by Jesus on the cross, which ones touch you the most? – Why?

LESSON

† 106. *What is the mystery of the Redemption?*

The mystery of the Redemption is the mystery of Jesus Christ dying on the cross to redeem all men.

• 107. *Did Jesus truly redeem all men?*

Yes, Jesus Christ truly redeemed all men, for by His life, His sufferings and His death, He earned for them forgiveness of their sins and the graces necessary to obtain heaven.

> NOTE: Jesus Christ was able to suffer because He is man, but His sufferings and His death have an infinite value because He is God.

- 108. *What did Jesus Christ suffer to redeem us?*

To redeem us, Jesus Christ suffered a cruel agony. He was betrayed by Judas, crowned with thorns, and condemned by Pontius Pilate. At last He died nailed to a cross.

NOTE: Yet the greatest suffering of Jesus Christ during the Passion was to feel Himself crushed, as it were, beneath the great number and the ugliness of our sins, and by the ingratitude of men.

- 109. *Why did Jesus Christ wish to suffer so much?*

Jesus Christ wished to suffer in order to show us better His love and to give us a greater horror for sin.

† 110. *Where and when did Jesus Christ die?*

Jesus Christ died in Jerusalem, on Calvary, on Good Friday, around three o'clock in the afternoon.

NOTE: To be sure that Jesus was dead, a soldier pierced His heart with a blow of the lance.

111. *What is meant by the words: "was buried"?*

By the words "was buried," is meant that after the death of Jesus Christ, His body was removed from the cross and placed in the tomb.

NOTE: Jesus was taken down from the cross by His friends. One of them, Joseph of Arimathea, gave a tomb which he owned, very near to Calvary, for the burial of Jesus.

112. *What is meant by the words: "He descended into hell"?*

By the words "He descended into hell," is meant that after the death of Jesus Christ, His soul went down to Limbo to visit the souls of the just who had died since the time of Adam, and to announce to them that they would soon enter into heaven.

> FOR MY LIFE – Every time I meet a procession following a cross or whenever I pass a shrine of the crucifixion, I will take my hat off with respect, aware that I am honoring the sign of my Redemption.
>
> I will do everything possible to make sure that the crucifix is given a place of honor in my home.
>
> PRAYER – "We adore Thee, O Christ, and we bless Thee, because by Thy holy cross Thou hast redeemed the world."
>
> THE WORD OF GOD – "I am the Good Shepherd…. I lay down My life for My sheep." (John 10:15-16)

The Mystery of the Redemption

Liturgy – Holy Week reminds us of the great mysteries of the Passion and death of Our Lord Jesus Christ.

The principal days of that week are: Palm Sunday, which celebrates the triumphal entry of Jesus into Jerusalem. The priest wears purple vestments. The faithful bring blessed palms back to their homes.

Holy Thursday: the anniversary of the institution of the Eucharist. Mass is celebrated with white vestments and with great solemnity.

On Good Friday, the priest wears black vestments. On that day there takes place the adoration of the cross as well as the liturgy of the Passion and death of Our Lord Jesus Christ.

On Holy Saturday, the Church blesses the new fire, the Paschal candle, and the baptismal water. At Mass, the priest wears white vestments.

Assignment – What did Judas do during the Passion of Jesus? – The Jews? – Saint Peter? – Caiphas? – Pilate? – The good thief? – The centurion?

Project – Compose a series of little drawings or little stained-glass windows representing the stations of the Way of the Cross.

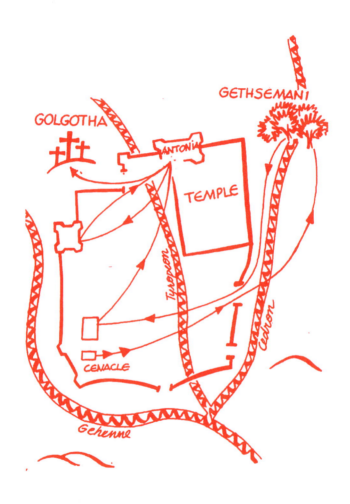

LESSON 15

THE FIFTH ARTICLE OF THE CREED:

"...On the third day He rose again from the dead."

THE RESURRECTION OF OUR LORD JESUS CHRIST

The Jews placed soldiers around the sepulcher of Jesus; then they put a seal on the stone.

On the third day, the holy women left before dawn to pour perfumes on the body of Jesus. On the way there, they were saying to each other: "Who shall roll us back the stone from the door of the sepulcher?" When they arrived, they saw the sepulcher empty, and an angel said to them: "Be not affrighted, you seek Jesus of Nazareth, Who was crucified. He is risen: He is not here. Go, tell His disciples and Peter that He goeth before you into Galilee. There you shall see him, as He told you."[12]

Then Peter and John ran to the tomb and saw that Jesus was indeed no longer there. The Master appeared to Mary Magdalen and then to two disciples on the road to Emmaus. Finally, He appeared to the Apostles, when Thomas was not there.

When Thomas returned, the other disciples said to him: "We have seen the Lord"; but he said to them: "Except I shall see in His hands the print of the nails and put my finger into the place of the nails and put my hand into His side, I will not believe."

Eight days later, the disciples were again gathered together and Thomas was with them. Jesus came, though the doors were closed, and He stood in the midst of them and said: "Peace be to you." He then turned to Thomas and said to him: "Put in thy finger hither and see My hands. And bring hither thy hand and put it into My side. And be not faithless, but believing." Thomas answered: "My Lord and my God." Jesus said to him: "Because thou has seen Me, Thomas, thou hast believed: blessed are they that have not seen and have believed."[13]

REVIEW – By whom was the tomb guarded? – What did the holy women say on the way to the tomb? – What did they see when they arrived? – Which Apostles ran to the tomb? – What did Saint Thomas say when the Apostles told him: "We have seen Jesus"? – What happened?

---

[12] Mark 16:1-7
[13] John 20:19-29

The Resurrection of Our Lord Jesus Christ

LESSON

† 113. *On what day did Jesus Christ rise from the dead?*

Jesus Christ rose from the dead on the third day after His death, on Easter day.

> **NOTE: Jesus Christ had foretold His resurrection when He said, speaking of His body: "Destroy this temple; and in three days I will raise it up." (John 2:19)**

• 114. *Are we certain that Jesus Christ is risen from the dead?*

Yes, we are certain that Jesus Christ is risen from the dead because, after His death, His disciples saw Him living, they touched Him, spoke to Him, ate with Him and died to affirm His resurrection.

• 115. *What did Jesus do after His resurrection?*

After His resurrection, Jesus Christ remained forty more days on earth, to complete the instruction of the Apostles, and to prepare them to preach the Gospel.

> **FOR MY LIFE** – In reciting the "I believe in God," I will pay attention to these words: "He rose again from the dead," and I will think about the fact that the Apostles gave their lives to affirm the Resurrection. I will believe in men who allow themselves to be killed.
>
> **PRAYER** – O Lord, make me resurrect to a new life with Christ.
>
> **THE WORD OF GOD** – "If Christ be not risen again, your faith is vain." (Saint Paul, I Cor. 15:17)

LITURGY – The Feast of Easter recalls the resurrection of Our Lord Jesus Christ. This feast can vary from March 22nd to April 25th.

Eastertide lasts from Holy Saturday (at noon) until the end of the week following Pentecost. The liturgical color of this season is white or gold.

ASSIGNMENT – Was the tomb of Jesus well guarded? – To whom did Jesus appear? – Do you know which Apostle betrayed Him? – What day recalls the resurrection of Our Lord?

PROJECT – Draw an empty tomb.

Lesson 16

The Sixth and Seventh Articles of the Creed:

"...He ascended into heaven, is seated at the right hand of God, the Father Almighty, from thence He shall come to judge the living and the dead..."

The Ascension

Jesus had been risen from the dead for forty days. He had often shown Himself to His Apostles, continuing to teach them. On that final day, He again appeared, sat down at table with them and urged them not to leave Jerusalem, but to wait for what the Father had promised, that is to say, for the third Person of the Holy Trinity: the Holy Ghost. Then He led them to the Mount of Olives. "But you shall receive the power of the Holy Ghost coming upon you," He told them, "and you shall be witnesses unto Me in Jerusalem, and in all Judea, and Samaria, and even to the uttermost part of the earth." After He had finished speaking, He was lifted up to heaven in their presence and a cloud hid Him from their sight. Jesus had ascended into heaven.

Yet the Apostles had their eyes fixed on the place where the Master had disappeared; they looked and looked, trying to see Him. Then two angels clothed in white robes appeared before them and said to them: "Ye men of Galilee, why stand you looking up to heaven? This Jesus Who is taken up from you into heaven, shall so come as you have seen Him going into heaven."[14]

They then returned to Jerusalem and went into the Cenacle, or Upper Room, where they usually stayed, and there they began to pray. The Most Blessed Virgin Mary was there with them, along with some other people.

A short time after, Peter suggested to the Apostles and to the disciples who were there (they were about one hundred twenty people) that they choose a replacement for the traitor Judas, who had hanged himself after his crime.

They drew lots and it was Matthias who was chosen to be associated with the eleven Apostles.

REVIEW – What did Jesus urge His Apostles to do? – Where did He lead them on the fortieth day after His resurrection? – What did He say to them on the road? – What happened after He had spoken? – What did the two angels say to the Apostles? – To what place did the Apostles then withdraw? – Who was with them there? – What did Saint Peter do?

---

[14] Acts 1:8-10

LESSON

† 116. *On what day did Jesus ascend into heaven?*

Jesus Christ ascended into heaven on the day of the Ascension, forty days after His resurrection.

• 117. *Why did Jesus ascend into heaven?*

Jesus ascended into heaven to prepare a place for us there and to send us the Holy Ghost.

118. *What is meant by the words: "is seated at the right hand of God, the Father Almighty"?*

These words, "is seated at the right hand of God, the Father Almighty" mean that Jesus Christ, as God, is in heaven the equal of His Father, and that, as man, He is above all the angels and saints.

• 119. *What is meant by the words: "from thence He shall come to judge the living and the dead"?*

These words, "from thence He shall come to judge the living and the dead," mean that at the end of the world Jesus Christ will return visibly to the earth to judge all men.

> **FOR MY LIFE** – Jesus has ascended into heaven. I will see Him there one day if I do all that He asked me to do.
>
> **PRAYER** – "Grant, we beseech Thee, almighty God: that we, who believe Thine only begotten Son, our Redeemer, to have ascended on this day into heaven, may also ourselves dwell in mind amid heavenly things."
>
> **THE WORD OF GOD** – "I came forth from the Father and am come into the world: again I leave the world and I go to the Father." (John 16:28)

LITURGY – The Feast of the Ascension celebrates the day when Jesus ascended into heaven. It is one of the six holy days of obligation (in the United States).

The vestments are white or gold. At the High Mass, after the Gospel, the great Paschal candle is extinguished to recall that Jesus was lifted up into heaven.

ASSIGNMENT – Had Jesus foretold His ascension? – Where did it take place? – How many days was it after His resurrection? – Where is Jesus now? – Will He come back to earth one day? – When?

PROJECT – Using colored paper, make a stained-glass window representing the Ascension.

LESSON 17

EIGHTH ARTICLE OF THE CREED:

"...I believe in the Holy Ghost..."

THE HOLY GHOST

After the Ascension, the Apostles, gathered in the Upper Room, awaited the coming of the Holy Ghost. They had been there for ten days when, all of a sudden, a violent wind shook the house and they heard a great noise. At the same moment, tongues of fire appeared, which divided and settled over the head of each one of them. All were filled with the Holy Ghost.

Immediately, they began to speak different languages. A complete change had just come over their soul. They no longer feared the Jews; they understood everything Jesus had taught them, and they had only one desire: to speak of Jesus.

In Jerusalem on that day, in addition to the inhabitants, there were also many Jews from all different countries who had come for the Jewish feast of Pentecost. They ran toward the great noise which they had heard coming from the Upper Room. They were astonished when they heard the Apostles, full of joy, speaking their own languages, and they wondered what it all meant. Others made fun of the Apostles. Then Saint Peter stepped forward with the eleven Apostles and he preached Jesus Christ for the first time. He said to them: "This is that which was spoken of by the prophet...: 'upon My servants indeed and upon My handmaids will I pour out in those days of My Spirit....' Ye men of Israel, hear these words: Jesus of Nazareth, a man approved of God among you by miracles and wonders and signs, which God did by Him, in the midst of you, as you also know: This same being delivered up...you by the hands of wicked men have crucified and slain. Whom God hath raised up, having loosed the sorrows of hell....You know what Jesus of Nazareth worked in the midst of you....This Jesus hath God raised again, whereof all we are witnesses."[15]

Peter spoke so well under the inspiration of the Holy Ghost that many believed after his discourse and three thousand Jews were baptized. The Church of Christ soon spread over all the earth. (From the Acts of the Apostles.)

REVIEW – What happened on the day of Pentecost? – What change occurred in the souls of the Apostles? – What did Peter say to the Jews gathered before the Upper Room? – What was the result of his preaching?

---

[15] Acts 2:14-32

LESSON

† 120. *Who is the Holy Ghost?*

The Holy Ghost is the third Person of the Holy Trinity, equal to the Father and the Son in all things.

> NOTE: It is Jesus Christ Who taught us that the Holy Ghost exists and that He acts in souls and in the Church.

† 121. *Did the Holy Ghost descend visibly upon the earth?*

Yes, the Holy Ghost descended visibly upon the earth on the day of the Baptism of Our Lord, in the form of a dove; and on the day of Pentecost, upon the Apostles, in the form of tongues of fire.

• 122. *What did the Holy Ghost do in the Apostles?*

The Holy Ghost filled the Apostles with understanding and courage to preach the Gospel and to establish the Church of Jesus Christ everywhere on earth.

• 123. *What does the Holy Ghost do in the Church?*

The Holy Ghost maintains the Church in the truth, directs Her, sanctifies Her and upholds Her in Her combats.

• 124. *What does the Holy Ghost do in coming to live in our souls?*

The Holy Ghost, in coming to live in our souls, gives us supernatural life and dwells in us to help us do good and avoid evil.

> **FOR MY LIFE** – The Holy Ghost transformed the souls of the Apostles. He made me into a child of God; He is capable of transforming me, as well.
>
> **PRAYER** – "Come, Holy Ghost, fill the hearts of Thy faithful and kindle in them the fire of Thy love."
>
> **THE WORD OF GOD** – "The Holy Ghost will teach you all things and bring all things to your mind, whatsoever I shall have said to you." (John 14:26)

Fear of the Lord — Wisdom — Understanding — Piety — Counsel — Knowledge — Fortitude

LITURGY – The Feast of Pentecost recalls the day when the Holy Ghost descended upon the Apostles. At the Mass of that feast, the Church makes known the effects that the Holy Ghost produced in the world and those that it should produce, in particular, in our souls.

The liturgical color is red.

ASSIGNMENT – On what day did the Holy Ghost descend on the Apostles? – How were they before the coming of the Holy Ghost? – How were they after? – When does the Holy Ghost come into a soul? – When does the Christian receive all of His gifts?

PROJECT – Draw a frieze representing the descent of the Holy Ghost and a construction representing the Upper Room.

Our Lord Jesus Christ Continues His Mission Through the Church

St. Peter's in Rome

LESSON 18

NINTH ARTICLE OF THE CREED

"...I believe in the Holy Catholic Church..."

THE CHURCH

After Peter said to Jesus: "You are Christ, the Son of the living God." Jesus, to show that He wished to establish Peter as the foundation of the whole Church, said to him: "Thou art Peter, and upon this rock I will build My Church, and the gates of hell shall not prevail against it." Next, to express the authority of the Apostle in another way, He added: "I will give to thee the keys of the kingdom of heaven. And whatsoever thou shalt bind upon earth, it shall be bound also in heaven: and whatsoever thou shalt loose on earth, it shall be loosed also in heaven."[16]

The verbs are in the future tense, meaning it is a promise. The day came when Jesus instituted that

---

[16] Matthew 16:18-19

society; He compared the head, Saint Peter, to a shepherd who is leading a flock.

REVIEW – Why are you a part of the true Church? – To what might you be compared? – To what might one compare the apostates, the excommunicated, etc.? – What did Jesus say about the infidels?

LESSON

125. *Is Our Lord still with us?*

Yes, Our Lord is still with us through the Church. She continues His mission by giving us His thought, His grace, and even His living Person.

THE CHURCH

† 126. *What is the Church?*

The Church is the society which unites all Christians to Jesus Christ, who founded It.

† 127. *Is the Church of this earth the only part of the Church?*

No, the Church of this earth is not the only part of the Church; It also includes all of the souls united to Jesus in the glory of Heaven (the Church Triumphant), and those who still suffer in Purgatory (the Church Suffering).

† 128. *Is the Church a visible society?*

The Church on this earth (the Church Militant) is a visible society governed by the Pope, and by the bishops united to the Pope. These are the faithful of the Church.

> NOTE: To be a true member of the Church, it is necessary to believe what It teaches, do what It commands, and receive Its sacraments.

129. *Who are those outside the Church?*

Those who are outside the Church are: the infidels, the apostates, the heretics, the schismatics and the excommunicated.

> NOTE: 1. An infidel is one who is not baptized and who does not believe in Jesus Christ.
>
> 2. And apostate is a baptized person who renounces the faith exteriorly after having received it and practiced it.
>
> 3. A heretic is a baptized person who obstinately refuses to believe a truth revealed by God and taught by the Church.
>
> 4. A schismatic is a baptized person who believes what the Church teaches but who refuses to obey Its leaders.
>
> 5. An excommunicate is a baptized person whom the Church or the Pope rejects from the society of the faithful, on account of his scandals.

130. *When did Jesus Christ name Saint Peter the head of His Church?*

Jesus Christ named Saint Peter the head of His Church when He said to him: "Thou art Peter; and upon this rock I will build My Church... I will give to thee the keys of the kingdom of heaven... Feed My lambs, feed My sheep," which is to say, be the leader of the shepherds and of the faithful.

> NOTE: The first two statements are in the future tense: They are promises. The third, which is in the present tense, is the realization of that promise; it was spoken by Jesus after His resurrection.

131. *Is it necessary to belong to the true Church?*

Yes, it is necessary to belong to the true Church, and those who willfully remain outside the Church cannot be saved.

LITURGY – O God, grant, we beseech Thee, that by both word and example the Pope may edify those whom he rules, and together with the flock committed to his care, may attain to eternal life.

Lesson 19

The Hierarchy of the Church

It was after the Resurrection. Jesus appeared to His Apostles on the shore of the lake and made Peter draw in a miraculous catch of one hundred and fifty-three big fish in his nets. After eating with His disciples, Jesus turned to Peter and said: "Simon, son of John, lovest thou Me more than these?" Peter answered: "Yea Lord, Thou knowest that I love Thee." Jesus said: "Feed My lambs." A second time He asked Peter the same question, received the same response, and said to him again: "Feed my lambs."

For the third time, Jesus asked the same thing. Then Peter, very moved, replied to Him: "Lord, Thou knowest all things: thou knowest that I love Thee." Jesus then said to him: "Feed My sheep."[17]

The Church now had a leader, and Jesus, Who had foreseen everything, before He ascended into heaven could send His Apostles to conquer the world, telling

---

[17] John 21:15-17

them: "Going therefore, teach ye all nations: baptizing them in the name of the Father and of the Son and of the Holy Ghost, teaching them to observe all things whatsoever I have commanded you. And behold I am with you all days, even to the consummation of the world."[18]

REVIEW – What did Jesus say to Peter, who had just affirmed his faith in the divinity of Christ? – How can you see: 1. That these words are a promise? 2. That they indicate a supreme authority? – At what moment and with what words did Jesus found His Church?

LESSON _____

THE POPE

† 132. *Who is the Pope?*

The Pope is the successor of Saint Peter, the representative of Jesus Christ, and the visible head of the Church.

> NOTE: The Pope is called the "Holy Father." He is indeed the father of all the bishops and all the faithful.

133. *What are the powers of the Pope?*

The powers of the Pope are to teach and to govern the entire Church, and to judge the pastors and the faithful.

---

[18] Matthew 28:19-20

- 134. *Can the Pope be mistaken?*

No, the Pope cannot be mistaken when he teaches the entire Church, as the successor of Peter, what it is necessary to believe and what it is necessary to do in order to go to heaven. He is then infallible.

135. *What are the duties of the pastors and the faithful toward the Pope?*

The duties of the pastors and the faithful toward the Pope are to love him as a father and obey him in all that he commands in the name of Jesus Christ.

THE BISHOPS

† 136. *Who are the Bishops?*

The Bishops are the successors of the Apostles, charged by the Pope with governing the dioceses.

> NOTE: A diocese is a certain expanse of land confided to a single Bishop.

137. *When were the Apostles and their successors appointed pastors of the Church?*

The Apostles and their successors were appointed pastors of the Church when Jesus Christ said to them: "Going, teach ye all nations: baptizing them in the name of the Father and of the Son and of the Holy Ghost....And behold I am with you all days, even to the consummation of the world."

- **138.** *By whom are the Bishops assisted in their apostolate?*

The Bishops are assisted in their apostolate by priests, and especially pastors placed by the Bishops at the head of parishes.

THE FAITHFUL

139. *What are the duties of the faithful toward the Bishops and the priests?*

The duties of the faithful toward the Bishops and the priests are to respect them, to obey them, and to help them in their apostolate.

140. *How should the faithful help their pastors in their apostolate?*

The faithful should help their pastors in their apostolate by praying for them, by being apostles under their direction, and by paying tithes.

> NOTE: The tithe is the annual contribution due by the faithful, for the support of the clergy. This contribution is obligatory because justice and gratitude make it a duty. Each ought to contribute to the support of the clergy according to his means.

FOR MY LIFE – I will have the greatest respect for the Pope, the Bishops, and the priests. I will help them and pray for them.

PRAYER – Lord, grant us priests; grant us many holy priests, and make us docile to their teaching.

THE WORD OF GOD – "All power is given to Me in heaven and on earth. Going, teach ye all nations, teaching them to observe all things whatsoever I have commanded you." (Matthew 28:19-20)

LITURGY – On June 29th, the Church celebrates the Feast of the Apostles Saint Peter and Saint Paul, martyred on the same day during the persecution of Nero, in Rome, where they had established the Church of Jesus Christ. The liturgy of this feast shows the primacy of Saint Peter.

The liturgical vestments are red.

ASSIGNMENT – Who is the present Pope? – What do you know of him? – Where does he live? – Who chooses the Pope? – How? – Who is your Bishop? – Have you assisted at a ceremony presided by him? – What did you notice?

PROJECT – Draw a miter or cut one out of cardstock. Draw a map of your diocese.

LESSON 20

THE MARKS OF THE TRUE CHURCH

Jesus founded a Church, that is to say a perfect society.

He did not found two or three, but one only. He said: "I will build My Church." He gave Her a single head. "Thou art Peter, and upon on this rock..." He gave only one doctrine: "Go, teach them to observe all things whatsoever I have commanded you."[19]

This Church was founded by Christ, whose sanctity has never been attacked by anyone. He alone was able to say to His enemies: "Which of you shall convince Me of sin?"[20] His doctrine is capable of forming saints: "Be you perfect, as also your heavenly Father is perfect," said Jesus.[21]

This Church was not for one or two races, but for all: "Go, teach all nations; preach the Gospel to every creatures..."

---

[19] Matthew 28:20
[20] John 8:46
[21] Matthew 5:48

Finally, to whom did Jesus say: "I am with you until the consummation of the world"? It was to His Apostles. Now, these men could not remain forever on earth, so this statement is made to the legitimate successors of the Apostles and to no others.

The true Church of Jesus is therefore the one which can be traced back to the Apostles.

You are going to see in the lesson you are about to study that you are part of the true Church.

REVIEW – What words show: That Jesus founded only one Church? – That this Church is holy? – That It is for all races? – To whom did Jesus say: "I am with you until the consummation of the world"?

LESSON

† 141. *Did Jesus Christ found several churches?*
No, Jesus Christ founded only one Church.

• 142. *By what marks can the true Church be recognized?*
The true Church can be recognized by four marks: It is one, holy, catholic, and apostolic.

143. *Which is the Church that possesses these four marks?*
The Church which possesses these four marks is the Roman Church.

> NOTE: The Church is called Roman because the Pope, Her visible head, is the bishop of Rome.

144. *Is the Roman Church "one"?*

Yes, the Roman Church is "one" because the Christians who make it up believe the same truths, receive the same sacraments, and obey the same head who is the Pope.

145. *Is the Roman Church holy?*

Yes, the Roman Church is holy:
- 1st Because Jesus Christ, Its founder, is holy;
- 2nd Because Its doctrine and Its sacraments are holy;
- 3rd Because It has always formed Saints.

146. *Is the Roman Church catholic, that is to say, universal?*

Yes, the Roman Church is catholic, that is to say, universal, because It was founded for men of all times and all countries.

147. *Is the Roman Church apostolic?*

Yes, the Roman Church is apostolic:
- 1st Because Its first heads were the Apostles;
- 2nd Because It is governed by the successors of the Apostles;
- 3rd Because It believes and teaches the doctrine of the Apostles.

> **FOR MY LIFE** – I will love the Church from whom I received supernatural life and who is therefore a Mother for me. I will defend Her if anyone attacks Her in my presence.
>
> **PRAYER** – "Lord, convert the heretics, the sinners and the infidels."
>
> **THE WORD OF GOD** – "The powers of hell shall not prevail against My Church." (Matthew 16:18)

LITURGY – The Church of Jesus Christ has formed saints everywhere. Thus, throughout the entire year She celebrates feasts in honor of the saints of all nations, both men and women.

Each parish ought to celebrate the feast of its patron saint in a special way. You know the great saints of France: Saint Martin of Tours, Saint Remigius, Saint Bernard, Saint Louis, Saint Vincent de Paul, the Curé of Ars, Saint Genevieve, Saint Clotilda, Saint Joan of Arc, Saint Theresa of the Child Jesus, Saint Bernadette and the saints of your diocese. [You know the great saints of England and America: Saint Augustine of Canterbury, Saint Thomas More, Saint John Fisher, Saint John Neumann, Saint Martin de Porres, Saint Rose of Lima, Saint Kateri Tekakwitha, Saint Elizabeth Ann Seton, Saint Francis Xavier Cabrini and the patron saint of your diocese.]

ASSIGNMENT – Are there many saints in the Church? – List those you know. – Has the true Church spread over the entire world? – What language manifests the unity of the Church? – Which are the churches that have broken away from the true Church of Jesus Christ?

PROJECT – Make an album with pictures cut out from newspapers or reviews representing the diverse activities of the Church in various countries (teaching, liturgical ceremonies, charitable or social works), in order to show Her unity, or else design friezes or models representing a scene from the life of the greatest saints (a saint for every century or for every country).

Lesson 21

The Faithful of the Church

You are part of the true Church of Jesus Christ because you have been baptized. You believe in the teaching of Christ, and you are subject to Its legitimate pastors. You are therefore in the field of the Good God like a good grain of wheat. But is there only good grain?

Jesus once said: A man had sown good grain in his field. However, while his servants were sleeping, his enemy came and sowed cockle, or weeds, throughout the field, along with the wheat, and then left.

When the plants had shot up leaves and the fruit had formed, the weeds appeared also. The servants told the master what had happened, and he answered: "An enemy hath done this." The servants said to him: "Wilt thou that we go and gather it up?" He told them: "No, lest perhaps gathering up the cockle, you root up the wheat together with it. Suffer both to grow until the harvest, and in the time of the harvest I will say to the reapers: gather up first the cockle, and bind it into bundles to burn, but the wheat gather ye into my barn." [22]

The weeds, the bad grain, are the apostates, the excommunicated, the heretics, the schismatics – all those who are in revolt against the law of God. But as long as they are on earth, they may convert and become good grain.

As for the infidels, who are not baptized, Jesus was speaking of them when He said: "Other sheep I have that are not of this fold; them also I must bring, and they shall hear My voice, and there shall be one fold and one shepherd."

God desires the salvation of all men.

REVIEW – What makes you a part of the true Church? To what might you be compared? To what might apostates, the excommunicated, etc., be compared? What did Jesus say about the infidels?

LESSON

• 148. *Whom do we call "the faithful of the Church"?*

We call "the faithful of the Church" the Christians subject to the Pope and the Bishops.

149. *Who are those outside the Church?*

Those who are outside the Church are the infidels, the apostates, the heretics, the schismatics, and the excommunicated.

---

[22] Matthew 13:24-30

NOTE: 1. An infidel is one who is not baptized and who does not believe in Jesus Christ.

2. An apostate is a baptized person who renounces the faith exteriorly after having received it and practiced it.

3. A heretic is a baptized person who obstinately refuses to believe a truth revealed by God and taught by the Church.

4. A schismatic is a baptized person who believes what the Church teaches but who refuses to obey Its leaders.

5. An excommunicate is a baptized person whom the Church or the Pope rejects from the society of the faithful, on account of his scandals.

150. *Is it necessary to belong to the true Church?*

Yes, it is necessary to belong to the true Church, and those who willfully remain outside the Church cannot be saved.

FOR MY LIFE – I will think of all those who do not have the happiness of being Christians, and for whom Christ died, since He died for all men. I will ask God to give them the grace to be saved, and for that I will offer my work and my sacrifices.

PRAYER – "Thy kingdom come."

THE WORD OF GOD – "And other sheep I have that are not of this fold: them also I must bring." (John 10:16)

LITURGY – In the prayers of Good Friday, the celebrant prays in the name of the Church for the Pope, the Bishops, the priests, deacons, subdeacons, clerics, confessors, virgins, widows, and all the people of God; for the catechumens; for an end of all errors, of all evils; for heretics and schismatics, for the faithless Jews and for the pagans.

ASSIGNMENT – Are there still many men who do not know Jesus Christ? – Whose mission is it to teach them about the Savior? – Are they numerous? – What can you do to help them?

PROJECT – Our Lord compared the Church to a tree. Draw a tree with its branches where sap is flowing (the faithful) and those which have broken off from the trunk in the course of the centuries. Build a series of dioramas on the principal activities of the missionary apostolate.

Lesson 22

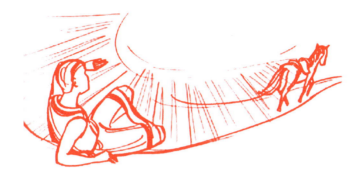

The Ninth Article of the Creed

"...I believe in the Communion of Saints"

The Communion of Saints

Saint Stephen, as he was stoned by the Jews, was praying for his executioners. The man who was to become Saint Paul was watching him die. What was the effect of the martyr's prayer? You are going to find out. You know the story of the conversion of Saint Paul. At that time he was breathing out only threatenings and slaughter against the disciples of Jesus Christ. He was on his way to find the high priest, in order to obtain permission to bring the Christians of Damascus as prisoners to Jerusalem.

He was on the road which leads to that town, when all of a sudden he was surrounded by a light from heaven. He fell to the ground and heard a voice saying to him: "Saul, Saul, why persecutest thou Me?" He answered: "Who art thou, Lord?" and the Lord said to him: "I am Jesus Whom thou persecutest."[23]

Saint Paul had been conquered; he had converted. Notice, however, what Jesus said: "Thou persecutest Me." In fact, he was persecuting Christians: men, women, old people, and children. Yet, Jesus was speaking truly: all Christians are one with Him. After he had converted, the apostle Saint Paul explained it in this way to the faithful: "For as the body is one and hath many members; and all the members of the body, whereas they are many, yet are one body: so also is Christ....Now you are the body of Christ and members of member."[24]

So we are indeed united in Jesus, as united as the vine and the branches of a grapevine, as united as the members of one body, through which there flows the same blood.

REVIEW – What was Paul going to do at Damascus? – What happened to him on the road? – What do you notice in Jesus' words? – How did Saint Paul explain the same thing to the faithful?

LESSON

- 151. *What does "the Communion of Saints" mean?*

"The Communion of Saints," means that the members of the Church are united to one another.

---

[23] Acts 9:1-18
[24] I Corinthians 12:12, 27

The Communion of Saints

- 152. *Who are the members of the Church united by the Communion of Saints?*

The members of the Church united by the Communion of Saints are: the Saints in heaven, the souls in purgatory, and the faithful on earth.

> NOTE: The Saints in heaven are called the Church Triumphant; the souls in purgatory, the Church Suffering; and the faithful on earth, the Church Militant.
>
> All of these members form a single Church: the Church of Jesus Christ.
>
> Together they form a single body, which we call the Mystical Body of Christ.

153. *How are you united to the Saints in heaven?*

I am united to the Saints in heaven by the prayers which I address to them and by the graces which they obtain for me from God.

154. *How are you united to the souls in purgatory?*

I am united to the souls in purgatory by the prayers and the good works which I offer to God for their relief.

> NOTE: We must have Masses said for the souls in purgatory because the sacrifice of Christ is the most powerful prayer to release them from suffering.

155. *How are the faithful on earth united to one another?*

The faithful on earth are united to one another because each one benefits from the prayers and merits of all.

NOTE: The merits of Jesus Christ, of the Blessed Virgin and of the Saints, the Sacrifice of the Mass, the sacraments, and the good works of the faithful constitute what are called the spiritual goods of the members of the Church. These goods are available to all.

FOR MY LIFE – I will think about how everyone benefits if I do good; and if I do evil, how everyone suffers.

I will also think about the fact that the Church is not only the Church on earth. I will call upon the Saints in heaven; I will pray for the souls in purgatory.

PRAYER – "O Lord, pour forth Your blessings on my parents, my benefactors, my friends and my enemies."

"O God of goodness and mercy, have pity also on the souls of the faithful who are in purgatory. Give them rest and eternal light."

THE WORD OF GOD – "Now you are the body of Christ and members of member." (I Cor. 12:27)

LITURGY – On November 1st, the Church celebrates the Feast of All Saints, to honor all of the Saints in heaven on the same day. It is one of the six holy days of obligation (in the United States).

ASSIGNMENT – Quote something Jesus said which proves that He loved little children – and the poor – and the sick.

The Communion of Saints

Project – Illustrate with a drawing the comparisons used by Our Lord and by Saint Paul to symbolize the unity of the Mystical Body.

Lesson 23

Tenth Article of the Creed

"...I believe in the forgiveness of sins."

The Forgiveness of Sins

You have seen that Our Lord compared the faithful to sheep. He said that He was the good shepherd who gives His life for them. He loved them all, the sheep who stay in the sheepfold as well as those who wander away. For this reason, sinners drew near to Him and the Pharisees murmured against Him, saying: "This man receiveth sinners and eateth with them."

Then Jesus told them this parable: "What man of you that hath an hundred sheep, and if he shall lose one of them, doth he not leave the ninety-nine in the desert and go after that which was lost, until he find it? And when he hath found it, lay it upon his shoulders, rejoicing? And coming home, call together his

The Forgiveness of Sins

friends and neighbors, saying to them: 'Rejoice with me, because I have found my sheep that was lost'?

"And I say to you that even so there shall be joy in heaven upon one sinner that doth penance, more than upon ninety-nine just who need not penance."[25]

You can understand why we recite: "I believe in the forgiveness of sins."

Jesus gave the means to take away sins. You are going to see it in this lesson.

REVIEW – What comparisons did Jesus use in speaking of the faithful? – With what did the Pharisees reproach Him? – What does the parable of the lost sheep prove?

LESSON

156. *When did Jesus Christ give to His Church the power to forgive all sins?*

Jesus Christ gave to His Church the power to forgive all sins on the evening of His resurrection.

† 157. *How does the Church forgive sins?*

The Church forgives sins principally by the sacraments of Baptism and Penance.

---

[25] Luke 15:1-7

> **FOR MY LIFE** – I have so many sins to be forgiven! I will forgive others so that God will forgive me and I will never hold a grudge against anyone at all.
>
> **PRAYER** – "Forgive us our trespasses as we forgive those who trespass against us."
>
> **THE WORD OF GOD** – "The Son of Man is come to seek and to save that which was lost." (Luke 19:10)

LITURGY – The blessing of the baptismal water takes place during the Vigil, that is to say on the eve, of Easter (and formerly of Pentecost). The celebrant blesses the water which will be used for Baptism, the sacrament which takes away Original Sin.

ASSIGNMENT – Name the sinners whom Jesus forgave in the Gospel. – Who was surprised one day at seeing Him forgive sins? – Who did He have to be, in order to forgive sins? – To whom did He give the power to forgive sins?

PROJECT – Make a series of friezes or dioramas on the parables in which Jesus expressed how He felt toward sinners (especially the sterile fig tree – the lost sheep – the lost drachma – the prodigal son).

What Jesus Christ Taught Us About Eternal Life

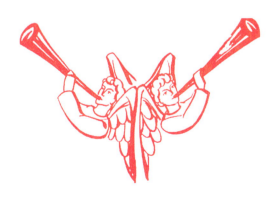

Lesson 24

Eleventh and Twelfth Articles of the Creed

"I believe in the resurrection of the body and life everlasting"

Life Everlasting

You know what death is. You should also know where it leads you. Read this parable:

There was a rich man, clothed in purple and linen, who feasted every day. Now, a poor man named Lazarus, who was covered with sores, lay near his door. He longed to gather what fell from the table of the rich man. Dogs would pass by and lick his wounds.

A day came when the poor man died and was carried by angels up to Abraham. The rich man also died and was buried. From the dwellings of the dead, in

LIFE EVERLASTING

the midst of tortures, he raised up his eyes and saw Abraham far off, and Lazarus in his bosom. "Father Abraham," he cried out, "have mercy on me and send Lazarus, that he may dip the tip of his finger in water to cool my tongue, for I am tormented in this flame."

"Son," said Abraham, "remember that thou didst receive good things in thy lifetime, and likewise Lazarus evil things: but now he is comforted and thou art tormented. And besides all this, between us and you, there is a great chaos: so that they who would pass from hence to you cannot, nor from thence hither."

"Then, father, I beseech thee," said the rich man, "that thou wouldst send him to my father's house, for I have five brethren, that he may testify unto them, lest they also come into this place of torments." "They have Moses and the prophets," said Abraham, "Let them hear them." "No, Father Abraham," he said, "but if one went to them from the dead, they will do penance." "If they hear not Moses and the prophets, neither will they believe, if one rise again from the dead." (Luke 16:19-31)

REVIEW – What did the rich man do? – What was the misery of poor Lazarus? – Where did Lazarus go when he died? – Where did the bad rich man go? – What did he ask? – What answer did he receive?

LESSON

• 158. *Is there another life after our life on earth?*

Yes, after our life on earth, there is another life, which will never end: it is eternal life.

I. Death

† 159. *What is death?*

Death is the separation of the soul from the body.

> NOTE: Jesus Christ asks us to think about death: "Watch ye therefore, because you know not the day nor the hour." (Matthew 25:13)

• 160. *What will become of our body after death?*

After death, our body will fall into dust, but it will rise again at the end of the world.

> NOTE: Our body will rise again at the end of the world in order to be rewarded or punished along with the soul.
>
> Jesus Christ foretold this resurrection: "The hour cometh wherein all that are in the graves shall hear the voice of the Son of God. And they that have done good things shall come forth unto the resurrection of life: but they that have done evil, unto the resurrection of judgment." (John 5:28-29)

II. The Particular Judgment

† 161. *What will become of our soul after death?*

After death our soul will appear before God in order to be judged for its good or bad actions. This is called the particular judgment.

† 162. *Where will our soul go after the particular judgment?*

After the particular judgment, our soul will go to purgatory, to heaven or to hell, according to its merits.

III. Purgatory

• 163. *What is purgatory?*

Purgatory is a place of suffering where the souls of the just finish expiating their sins before entering into heaven.

> NOTE: A soul which goes to purgatory is in the state of grace but is still guilty of venial sins, or has not done sufficient penance on earth.

IV. Heaven

• 164. *What is heaven?*

Heaven or paradise is a place of perfect happiness where the angels and the saints see God and possess Him forever.

> NOTE: It is certain that heaven exists since Jesus Christ often says so in the Gospel, and tells us what He will say to the good on the day of the general judgment: "Come, ye blessed of My Father, possess you the kingdom prepared for you from the foundation of the world."[26]

---

[26] Matthew 25:34

- 165. *Who are those who go to heaven?*

Those who go to heaven are those who die in the state of grace and who no longer have any punishment to suffer for their sins.

V. Hell

- 166. *What is hell?*

Hell is a place of torment where the wicked are forever separated from God and endure sufferings which will never end, alongside the devils.

NOTE: It is certain that hell exists, since Jesus Christ often says so in the Gospel, and tells us what He will say to the wicked on the day of the general judgment: "Depart from Me, you cursed, into everlasting fire, which was prepared for the devil and his angels."[27]

- 167. *Who are those who go to hell?*

Those who go to hell are those who die in a state of mortal sin.

VI. The General Judgment

168. *When will the last judgment, or general judgment, take place?*

The last judgment, or general judgment, will take place at the end of the world, when Jesus Christ returns visibly to earth to judge all men.

---

[27] Matthew 25:41

> **FOR MY LIFE** – Every evening I will make an examination of conscience, and I will not sleep before asking God's forgiveness for all my sins.
>
> **PRAYER** – Grant, O my God, that I may never forget that "one thing only is necessary" and that death "comes like a thief," as you have warned me.
>
> **THE WORD OF GOD** – "For what doth it profit a man, if he gain the whole world and suffer the loss of his own soul?" (Matthew 16:26)

LITURGY – On November 2nd, the Church celebrates the commemoration of the dead and invites all Christians to pray for the souls suffering in purgatory.

On that day priests may say three Masses, as on Christmas.

The liturgical vestments are black.

ASSIGNMENT – Do we know the hour of our death? – Did Jesus tell us that it would come as a surprise? – Did Jesus speak of heaven? – Quote one of His statements. – What did Jesus say about hell? – When one is in a state of grace, does one always go to heaven right away? – What must be done first? – Could one not expiate his sins before dying? How?

PROJECT – Illustrate with drawings, or make a stage with movable figures to show the parables about heaven (the marriage feast, the ten virgins, the weeds, the pearl, the talents, etc.)

SECOND PART

The Remedies Which Jesus Christ Prepared for Us

JESUS CHRIST SAID: "I AM…**THE LIFE**…"

*Jesus Christ brought us life.
The Church communicates to us this life of grace
through the Sacraments.*

Lesson 25

Grace in General

I. Sanctifying Grace

You know what a briar bush is: it is a wild rose tree. It only gives little flowers which are neither beautiful nor fragrant. It will stay that way for years and then it will die like all plants. But if a gardener tends to that briar bush, if he grafts the bud of a pretty rosebush under the bark, that same little briar bush receives a new life. It will produce beautiful, fragrant roses.

The briar bush did not do anything to change its natural life; it is the gardener who worked and if it now gives beautiful roses, it is because of the gardener.

Man was like that briar bush. He could not do anything to earn heaven. Jesus came like a divine gardener and He gave us the grace of God, so that we are now able to live as children of God and one day reach His heaven.

Sanctifying grace is the life of the Good God in us. To help us understand what this life is in us, Jesus used this comparison:

"I am the vine: you the branches." "Abide in Me: and I in you. As the branch cannot bear fruit of itself, unless it abide in the vine, so neither can you, unless you abide in Me."[28]

You have seen a grapevine before. Little branches with clusters of grapes grow out of the knotted vine; the fruits are only produced because of the sap which flows up the vine and into the branches. The life of God is that sap.

> Jesus is the vine.
>
> We are the little branches.
>
> The grape clusters are everything we do for heaven.

We need to explain the comparison: if the little branch were broken off and separated from the vine, would it still produce any grapes? No, because the sap would no longer be flowing through it. A soul which separates itself from God by mortal sin is a branch separated from the vine; it can no longer produce anything for heaven. Although a broken branch is no longer good for anything except to be burned, a soul in the state of mortal sin can be reattached to Jesus by perfect contrition or by the sacrament of Penance.

---

[28] John 15:5, 4

I. Sanctifying Grace

REVIEW – What grows on a briar that has never been tended? – What can grow on a grafted briar? – What could man do without Jesus? – What can he do with Jesus? – How many kinds of life do you have? – To what can you compare the sap, the vine, the branches, and the clusters of grapes?

LESSON

- 169. *Without the help of Jesus Christ can we live as Christians and go to heaven?*

No, without the help of Jesus Christ we cannot live as Christians and go to heaven, for He Himself said: "Without Me you can do nothing."

170. *How did Jesus Christ give us His help?*

Jesus Christ gives us His help through grace.

- 171. *What is grace?*

Grace is a supernatural gift which God grants to us out of pure goodness.

- 172. *How many kinds of grace are there?*

There are two kinds of grace: sanctifying or habitual grace and actual grace.

† 173. *What is sanctifying grace?*

Sanctifying grace is the gift of supernatural life which the three Divine Persons grant to us by coming to dwell in our soul.

NOTE: 1st Whoever has sanctifying grace possesses in his soul the Holy Trinity: the Father, the Son and the Holy Ghost.

"We will come to him and will make Our abode with him," said Jesus. [29]

2nd In coming to dwell within us, the Holy Trinity communicates to us a life like to Its own.

Jesus told us: "I am the true vine, you are the branches."[30]

As the sap flows from the vine into the branches and makes them bear fruit, so grace passes from God into us and gives us His life.

• 174. *What does supernatural life make of us?*

Supernatural life makes us adopted children of God, brothers of Jesus Christ, and living temples of the Holy Ghost.

175. *How is supernatural life given to us?*

Supernatural life is ordinarily given to us by Baptism, which is like a second birth for us.

† 176. *How does one lose supernatural life?*

One loses supernatural life by mortal sin.

• 177. *How can supernatural life be given back to us?*

Supernatural life can be given back to us by perfect contrition or by the sacrament of Penance.

---

[29] John 14:23
[30] John 15: 5

I. SANCTIFYING GRACE

> **FOR MY LIFE** – Every evening I will strive to have perfect contrition, to be sure of staying united to Jesus Christ.
>
> **PRAYER** – "My Lord, keep me in the state of grace."
>
> **THE WORD OF GOD** – "If thou didst know the gift of God." (John 4:10)

LITURGY – In the Gospel of Saint John, recited at the end of Mass, we are reminded that to all those who have believed in Him, the Son of God has given the power to become sons of God.

ASSIGNMENT – When did you receive sanctifying grace? – How can it increase? – How can it be lost? – When one has lost it, how can it be recovered? – Where does one go if he dies in the state of grace? Why? – Are we alone when we are in the state of grace? – Who dwells within us?

PROJECT – Make a little stage with clay characters to illustrate the conversation of Jesus with Nicodemus.

Lesson 26

II. Actual Grace

The Good God tends our soul as the vinedresser tends his grapevine. When the sap begins to rise, the vinedresser pulls out the weeds that are growing at the foot of the plant. He ties the grapevine to a little stake as soon as the leaves have sprouted; he sprays his vineyard to keep the plants from becoming sick.

God does the same thing for our soul. To allow us to do good, He gives us good thoughts, He shows us the ugliness of sin, and He strengthens our will. In a word, He gives us what are called actual graces.

However, while the grapevine has no choice but to let itself be tended, our soul can follow the grace of God or put up resistance. Saint Paul on the road to Damascus did not resist grace. As soon as Jesus had said: "Saul, why persecutest thou Me?" He answered: "Lord, what wilt thou have me to do?" Judas, on the contrary, resisted. In the Garden of Olives, when he came to betray his Master, Jesus said to him affec-

II. Actual Grace

tionately: "My friend..." But the traitor pushed away the thoughts of repentance which may have come into his soul; he willed to do evil...

To help us understand that God cares for sinful souls up to the very end, Jesus told this parable: "A certain man had a fig tree planted in his vineyard: and he came seeking fruit on it and found none. And he said to the dresser of the vineyard: 'Behold, for these three years I come seeking fruit on this fig tree and I find none. Cut it down therefore. Why cumbereth it the ground?' But he answering, said to him: 'Lord, let it alone this year also, until I dig about it and dung it. And if happily it bear fruit: but if not, then after that thou shalt cut it down.'"[31]

REVIEW – How does the vinedresser tend his vineyard? – How does God tend our souls? – Name a man who accepted the grace of God; name another who rejected it. – What is meant by the parable of the sterile fig tree?

LESSON

- 178. *What is actual grace?*

Actual grace is a temporary help which God gives, strengthening us to do good and avoid evil.

179. *Does God always give us the help we need in order to go to heaven?*

Yes, God always gives us the help we need in order to go to heaven.

---

[31] Luke 13:6-9

180. *Can we resist actual grace?*

Yes, we can resist actual grace by not following the good thoughts or the good desires which God gives to us.

181. *What do those risk who frequently resist actual grace?*

Those who frequently resist actual grace risk forming a habit of sin and losing heaven.

• 182. *What are the ordinary means by which Jesus Christ communicates His grace to us?*

The ordinary means by which Jesus Christ communicates His grace to us are prayer and the sacraments.

FOR MY LIFE – God never forces me to do good, but He enlightens me and He helps me. I should therefore ask Him for light and strength.

PRAYER – "O God, grant me light and strength to do good and avoid evil."

THE WORD OF GOD – "Without Me you can do nothing."

LITURGY – In the Gospel for the ninth Sunday after Pentecost, Jesus foretells the chastisement of the city of Jerusalem, which despised the grace of God.

ASSIGNMENT – What is the difference between actual grace and sanctifying grace? – Can sinners, pagans, or heretics receive actual graces? – Is grace always neces-

II. Actual Grace

sary in order to do good and avoid evil? – Is it necessary in order to be an apostle?

PROJECT – Illustrate with a shadow theater the miracle of the conversion of Saint Paul. Make a diorama representing Saint Peter walking on water.

Lesson 27

Prayer

A child is not afraid to speak to his father and to ask him for what he wants. We are the children of the Good God: let us behave as His children.

To show us what prayer can do, Jesus told the following parable: A man came to find his friend in the middle of the night, and since the door of the house was closed, he cried out: "Friend, lend me three loaves of bread, for one of my friends has arrived at my house on a voyage and I have nothing to offer him." From inside the house, the friend answered: "The door is closed, the whole house is sleeping, I cannot get up to give them to you." But the visitor insisted so much that his friend got up and gave him what he was asking, just so he could have peace.

Jesus then said: "And I tell you: ask and it shall be given to you, seek and you shall find, knock and the door will be opened unto you. For whoever asks, receives; and whoever seeks, finds; and to whoever knocks at the door it will be opened.

"If the son of one of you asks him for bread, will he give him a stone? Or if he asks for a fish, will he give him a serpent?

"If therefore you, wicked as you are, know how to give good things to your children, so much more your Father Who is in heaven will give good things to those who pray." (Luke 11)

REVIEW – What does the friend ask for who comes during the night? – What does the man in the house answer? – Why does the friend obtain what he was asking for? – How did Jesus explain this parable?

LESSON

† 183. *What does it mean to pray?*

To pray is to speak to God in order to adore Him, thank Him, ask Him for forgiveness, and obtain His graces.

• 184. *Are we obliged to pray?*

Yes, we are obliged to pray; it is a duty of which Jesus Christ often reminds us in the Gospel.

† 185. *When must we pray?*

We must pray often, but especially in the morning and evening, in temptation, and in trials and danger.

186. *For whom should we pray?*

We should pray for ourselves, for our parents and benefactors, for the heads of the Church, for the living and for the dead.

• 187. *How must we pray?*

We must pray with attention, humility, confidence, and perseverance.

> NOTE: Jesus said that "we ought always to pray, and not to faint." (Luke 18:1)

188. *Is it recommended that we pray with others?*

Yes, it is recommended that we pray with others, for Jesus Christ said: "Where there are two or three gathered together in My name, there am I in the midst of them."[32]

> NOTE: We pray in common at Church offices and in family prayer.

---

[32] Matthew 18:20

> **FOR MY LIFE** – I will not forget my morning and evening prayers and I will say them with great faith. Often during the day I will raise my heart to God by an ejaculatory prayer ("My God, I offer You this difficulty." – "My God, come to my assistance." – "My God, I love You," etc.).
>
> **PRAYER** – "Lord, teach us to pray."
>
> **THE WORD OF GOD** – "Amen, amen I say to you: if you ask the Father anything in My name, He will give it you. Hitherto you have not asked anything in My name. Ask and you shall receive." (John 16:23-24)

LITURGY – Remember that the official prayers of the Church, those which are found in Her liturgy, are those which are the best suited to the needs of our souls. Learn to understand them; learn to use your missal.

ASSIGNMENT – Did Jesus pray? – To Whom did He pray? – Do you know people in the Gospel who prayed to Him? – Name some of the prayers which He answered. – What did the Apostles ask Him when they saw Him praying?

PROJECT – Make a drawing to represent the scene where Jesus said: "Knock and it shall be opened unto you."

Lesson 28

The Our Father

You know by heart the prayer "Our Father." This lesson will explain the meaning of the words which make it up. It was given to us by Jesus, the Son of God made man: "Do not multiply words, as the heathens who imagine that in their much speaking they may be heard.

"Be not you therefore like to them for your Father knoweth what is needful for you, before you ask Him. Thus therefore shall you pray: Our Father, Who art in heaven, hallowed be Thy name. Thy kingdom come, Thy will be done, on earth as it is in heaven. Give us this day our daily bread. Forgive us our trespasses as we forgive those who trespass against us and lead us not into temptation, but deliver us from evil."

Then Jesus said, to explain what He had just taught them: "For if you will forgive men their offences, your heavenly Father will forgive you also your

THE OUR FATHER

offences. But if you will not forgive men, neither will your Father forgive you your offenses."[33]

The Apostles learned this prayer; they wrote it in the Gospel, and for twenty centuries all Christians have repeated it after them.

REVIEW – What advice did Jesus give to His Apostles on prayer? – What phrase from the "Our Father" did He explain to them? – Where is this prayer written down?

LESSON

• 189. *Which is the best prayer?*

The best prayer is the "Our Father," which Our Lord Jesus Christ Himself taught to us.

† 190. *Recite the "Our Father."*

Our Father, Who art in heaven,
   1 – hallowed be Thy name.
   2 – Thy kingdom come,
   3 – Thy will be done on earth as it is in heaven.
   4 – Give us this day our daily bread
   5 – and forgive us our trespasses as we forgive those who trespass against us,
   6 – and lead us not into temptation,
   7 – but deliver us from evil. Amen.

191. *Why do we call God "Father"?*

We call God "Father" because He created us in His image and He adopted us for His children at our Baptism.

---

[33] Matthew 6:7-15

NOTE: 1st We say "Our Father" and not "My Father," because we are all brothers, since we are all children of God.

2nd The "Our Father" contains seven requests: In the first three, we ask God that He might be known, loved and obeyed on earth as He is in heaven.

In the last four, we ask God for the bread of the body and the bread of the soul, the forgiveness of our sins, strength against temptations, and deliverance from all evil.

FOR MY LIFE – I will love above all other prayers this prayer which Jesus taught me and I will be attentive to the meaning of the words which I am pronouncing.

PRAYERS – "Our Father…"

THE WORD OF GOD – "Call none your father upon earth; for one is your Father, Who is in heaven." (Matthew 23:9)

LITURGY – The Pater Noster is recited during the most important part of the Mass: during the Canon, between the Consecration and the Communion.

At a Baptism, the godfather and godmother recite it for the child being baptized. After Confirmation, the bishop has the newly confirmed recite it.

ASSIGNMENT – What is this kingdom of God which we ask to "come"? – Can we work for the kingdom of God? In what way? – What exactly is the bread for which Jesus tells us to ask? – Will the forgiveness of our sins be granted unconditionally?

The Our Father

PROJECT – Illustrate each one of the requests of the Pater Noster.

Lesson 29

The Angelic Salutation

There are no words which give more pleasure to the Blessed Virgin than to repeat to her that she is the Mother of God. That is what we say to her in the "Hail Mary," since we take up the words that the angel Gabriel used on the day of the Annunciation: "Hail Mary, full of grace, the Lord is with thee. Blessed art thou among women," along with another salutation formed by the words of Saint Elizabeth, the cousin of the Blessed Virgin.

Mary, knowing that she was to be the Mother of God, wished to go before her divine Son was born and see her cousin Elizabeth, who was going to be the mother of Saint John the Baptist. Elizabeth lived in a town of Judea, in the mountains. Mary set out on the journey.

When she had reached the house of her cousin, Mary greeted Elizabeth. At the sound of Mary's voice, Elizabeth was filled with the Holy Ghost and cried out as the angel had already done: "Blessed art thou among women," but then she added: "and blessed is the fruit of thy womb. And whence is this to me, that the mother of my Lord should come to me?..." Mary answered her: "My soul doth magnify the Lord and my spirit hath rejoiced in God my Savior, because He hath regarded the humility of His handmaid; for behold from henceforth all generations shall call me blessed...."[34]

Yes, all generations have placed themselves under the protection of the Blessed Virgin Mary and have said repeatedly to her: "Holy Mary, Mother of God, pray for us sinners, now and at the hour of our death."

REVIEW – How did the Angel Gabriel greet Mary? – What did Elizabeth say to the Blessed Virgin? – What did Mary reply?

LESSON

● 192. *What is the prayer which we should recite with the greatest confidence, after the "Our Father"?*

The prayer which we should recite with the greatest confidence after the "Our Father," is the "Hail Mary," also called the "Angelic Salutation."

† 193. *Recite the "Angelic Salutation."*

Hail, Mary, full of grace; the Lord is with thee. Blessed art thou among women and blessed is the fruit of thy womb, Jesus. Holy Mary, Mother

---

[34] Luke 1:28-48

of God, pray for us sinners, now and at the hour of our death. Amen.

194. *Why is this prayer called the "Angelic Salutation"?*

This prayer is called the "Angelic Salutation" because it begins with the salutation which the Angel Gabriel addressed to the Blessed Virgin, on the day of the Annunciation.

> NOTE: 1st The words which follow the salutation of the Angel were spoken by Saint Elizabeth, cousin of the Blessed Virgin, on the day of the Visitation.
>
> 2nd The second part of the "Angelic Salutation" was composed by the Church.

195. *What are the three principal feasts of the Virgin Mary?*

The three principal feasts of the Virgin Mary are:
December 8th: the Immaculate Conception
March 25th: the Annunciation
August 15th: the Assumption

> NOTE: We also celebrate
>
> September 8th: the Nativity of the Blessed Virgin
> February 2nd: the Purification
> August 22nd: the Immaculate Heart of Mary

The Angelic Salutation

> **For my life** – I will not forget for a single day to recite at least one "Hail Mary" and I will get used to saying a decade of the rosary every day.
>
> **Prayer** – "Hail, Mary…"
>
> **The Word of God** – "Behold thy mother." (John 19:27).

We Pray to You

Give bread to the wretched,
And may their hearts
   be filled with God,
We pray you on our knees,
 O Mother, hear us.

Already here below,
   give God to us,
You will give Him to us
   in heaven,
We pray you on our knees,
O Mother, hear us.

Convert all sinners,
Bring them back to the
   sweet Savior,
We pray you on our knees,
O Mother, hear us.

Reveal to us the Charity
Which makes us live
   as Christians,
We pray you on our knees,
 O Mother, hear us.

Give bread to the wretched,
And may their hearts be
   filled with God,
We pray you on our knees,
 O Mother, hear us.

Already here below,
   give God to us,
You will give Him to us
   in heaven,
We pray you on our knees,
O Mother, hear us.

–Jean Servel, OMI

Liturgy – The rosary is the recitation of five decades of "Hail Marys." Each decade is preceded by an "Our Father" and ends with a "Glory be to the Father and to the Son and to the Holy Ghost." It begins with the "I believe in God…," the "Our Father," three "Hail Marys," and the "Glory Be…"

ASSIGNMENT – What is the rosary? – How long is a full rosary? – Which are the months specially consecrated to praying to the Most Blessed Virgin? – Which day of the week is the day of the Most Blessed Virgin? – What are the "associations" created specially for praying to the Most Blessed Virgin? – What is the scapular?

In your parish, is the Blessed Virgin invoked under a special title? Why?

Describe the chapel of the Blessed Virgin in your parish church.

In your missal, find as many feasts of the Blessed Virgin as you can.

PROJECT – Present the joyful, sorrowful and glorious mysteries using a sketch, a tapestry or embroidery.

Lesson 30

The Sacraments

We have two lives: the natural life which results from the union of the soul and the body, and the supernatural life which results from the union of the soul with God.

The Natural Life

God has ordered everything on earth for our natural life or the life of body and soul.

1st   We are born into the natural life.

2nd   We grow and are strengthened.

3rd   We take in food.

4th   We find remedies against illness.

5th   Finally the moment comes when the life of the earth ends for us.

The Supernatural Life

Jesus, the Son of God, prepared everything for our supernatural life or the life of the soul with God.

1st   We are born into the supernatural life by Baptism.

2nd We are strengthened by Confirmation.

3rd   We are nourished by the Body of Christ Himself.

4th   In Penance, we have the great remedy against the illnesses of the soul.

5th   At the moment of death, Extreme Unction takes away the remains of our sins and helps us stay faithful to the Good God until the very end.

The sacraments therefore accompany man from the cradle to the grave.

Man Lives in Society

The last two sacraments take these new needs into account.

Matrimony

will sanctify the union of man and woman and give them the graces they need for the duties of the family.

Holy Orders

will be the divine means established by Our Lord to consecrate the leaders of the Church, to create priests whose mission will be to distribute the sacraments.

The seven sacraments follow man throughout his earthly life and lead him to heaven.

THE SACRAMENTS

REVIEW – How many kinds of life do we have? – Compare natural life and supernatural life. – Which are the two sacraments designed for man's life in society?

LESSON _____

• 196. *What is a sacrament?*

A sacrament is a sensible sign instituted by Our Lord Jesus Christ to produce or increase grace.

NOTE: A sensible sign is a thing which we can see, hear or touch, and which makes us know another thing which we cannot see or hear or touch. For example, the water of Baptism is a sign: when we see it flowing, it tells us that the soul is purified of Original Sin, and that sanctifying grace is produced.

† 197. *How many sacraments are there?*

There are seven sacraments: Baptism, Confirmation, Holy Eucharist, Penance, Extreme Unction, Holy Orders, and Matrimony.

198. *Do those who receive a sacrament always receive grace?*

Yes, those who receive a sacrament always receive grace, provided they have the necessary dispositions.

• 199. *What sin does he commit who receives the sacraments without the necessary dispositions?*

He who receives the sacraments without the necessary dispositions commits a mortal sin which we call a sacrilege.

• 200. *Are there sacraments which can only be received once?*

Yes, there are sacraments which can only be received once: they are Baptism, Confirmation and Holy Orders.

> NOTE: One can only receive Baptism, Confirmation and Holy Orders once because they produce an indelible mark on the soul which is called a character.

> FOR MY LIFE – A sacrament is a holy thing, for its price was the Blood of Christ. I will approach the sacraments with a great respect.
>
> PRAYER – "Lord, grant that, by things visible, we may be drawn to the love of things invisible."
>
> THE WORD OF GOD – "Going therefore, teach ye all nations; baptizing them in the name of the Father and of the Son and of the Holy Ghost." (Matthew 28:19)

The Sacraments

LITURGY – The Ritual is a liturgical book which includes the prayers and instructions for the administration of the sacraments. It also contains rubrics for processions and blessings.

ASSIGNMENT – Classify in three columns the sacraments which can:

1. give grace	2. increase grace	3. give grace back to the soul
1. be received once	2. be received several times	3. be received often

PROJECT – Make a leaflet or a series of engravings on linoleum tile where every sacrament is represented by an object symbolizing it.

LESSON 31

JESUS CHRIST GIVES US SUPERNATURAL LIFE

BAPTISM

After Pentecost, the Apostles began to preach and to baptize.

One day, an angel of the Lord said to the deacon Philip: "Arise, go towards the south, to the way that goeth down from Jerusalem into Gaza." He rose up and went. Now, a chamberlain of the queen of Ethiopia and superintendent of all her treasures, who had come to Jerusalem to adore the Lord, was on his way home. He was reading the prophet Isaiah as he sat in his chariot.

The Spirit said to Philip: "Go near, and join thyself to this chariot." The deacon did so and, hearing the traveler reading the prophet, he asked him: "Thinkest thou that thou understandest what thou readest?" The man answered: "And how can I, unless some man show me?" And he invited Philip to climb into the chariot and sit next to him. He then read this passage: "He was led as a sheep to the slaughter; and like a lamb without voice before his shearer, so openeth He not His mouth." The chamberlain asked: "I beseech thee, of whom doth the prophet speak this?"

Then Philip explained to him that the prophet was speaking of Jesus, and he taught him the Gospel.

As they went along the road, they came to some water, and the chamberlain said: "See, here is water: what doth hinder me from being baptized?"

Philip answered: "If thou believest with all thy heart, thou mayest." The chamberlain said: "I believe that Jesus Christ is the Son of God." He made the carriage stop, both descended into the water, and Philip baptized him. As they came out of the water, the Spirit of the Lord carried Philip away, and the chamberlain did not see him anymore. Then he continued on his path, filled with joy.[35]

REVIEW – Whom did the deacon Philip meet on the road? – What was that man doing? – What did they say to one another? – What was the result of their conversation? – What happened to Philip?

LESSON

† 201. *What is Baptism?*

Baptism is a sacrament which takes away original sin, gives us supernatural life and makes us Christians, that is to say, disciples of Jesus Christ and children of God and of the Church.

---

[35] Acts 8:26-39

202. *Does Baptism take away the sins committed after the age of reason?*

Baptism takes away the sins committed after the age of reason, provided we regret them; it also eliminates all of the punishment due to these sins.

203. *When one cannot be baptized, can Baptism be replaced?*

Yes, when one cannot be baptized, Baptism can be replaced by martyrdom, which we call Baptism of blood, or by a perfect love of God, which we call Baptism of desire.

204. *Are parents obliged to have their children baptized as soon as possible after their birth?*

Yes, parents are obliged to have their children baptized as soon as possible after their birth.

- 205. *Who ordinarily gives Baptism?*

Priests ordinarily give Baptism, but in case of necessity, anyone can and ought to baptize.

- 206. *What must one do to give Baptism?*

To give Baptism, one must:
- 1st have the intention to baptize,
- 2nd (oneself) pour water on the forehead of the person being baptized,
- 3rd say as one is doing so: "I baptize you in the name of the Father and of the Son and of the Holy Ghost."

207. *Why are a godfather and a godmother given to the child being baptized?*

A godfather and a godmother are given to the child being baptized so that they might make the promises of Baptism in his name and watch over his Christian upbringing.

• 208. *What does the person who receives Baptism solemnly promise?*

The person who receives Baptism solemnly promises to believe in Jesus Christ, to practice His commandments, and to renounce sin and the devil.

209. *Why does the Church give a Saint's name to the person being baptized?*

The Church gives a Saint's name to the person being baptized so that he might have a protector who prays for him in heaven and a model whom he imitates on earth.

> **FOR MY LIFE** – I will find out the date of my Baptism and I will celebrate the anniversary of it every year, as the day of the greatest grace of all my life.
>
> **PRAYER** – "Grant me, O God, to prepare myself to renew with fervor the promises of my Baptism and always to remain faithful to them."
>
> **THE WORD OF GOD** – "Unless a man be born again of water and the Holy Ghost, he cannot enter into the kingdom of God." (John 3:5)

LITURGY – A baptismal font is a basin or a pool which contains water blessed on Holy Saturday or on the Saturday before Pentecost to administer Baptism. Baptismal fonts are often in a side chapel of a church.

ASSIGNMENT – Describe the baptismal font of your church. – When does the priest bless the water which is to be used at Baptism? – Have you ever been present at a Baptism? – If you have, describe what you noticed.

PROJECT – Make a model representing the baptismal font of your church or a diorama representing the baptism of the servant of Queen Candace by the deacon Philip.

LESSON 32

JESUS CHRIST STRENGTHENS OUR SUPERNATURAL LIFE

CONFIRMATION

Confirmation at the time of the Apostles

We find several passages referring to Confirmation in the Acts of the Apostles, the book which tells what happened after the Gospels: "Now when the Apostles, who were in Jerusalem, had heard that Samaria had received the word of God, they sent unto them Peter and John. Who, when they were come, prayed for them, that they might receive the Holy Ghost. For He was not as yet come upon any of them; but they were only baptized in the name of the Lord Jesus.

"Then Peter and John laid their hands upon them, and they received the Holy Ghost." (Acts 8:14-17)

Another part of the same book tells how Saint Paul came to Ephesus, after traveling throughout the upper coasts of Asia Minor. There, he found believers who had not yet received the Baptism of Jesus. He gave them Baptism and then he imposed his hands upon them; the Holy Ghost then came upon them, and they began to speak in different languages and to prophesy. They were about twelve in all. (Acts 19:1-7)

You, too, will receive the Holy Ghost on the day of your Confirmation. Read the lesson very attentively and answer the following questions:

REVIEW – Who administers the sacrament? – What did the Bishop do before the anointing? – Where did he anoint? – How did he do it? – What does he say while anointing? – Who are the people accompanying those to be confirmed? – What happens in the soul of these children? – May they receive the sacrament again next year? Why?

LESSON

† 210. *What is Confirmation?*

Confirmation is a sacrament which gives us the Holy Ghost with the superabundance of His gifts, to make us perfect Christians, witnesses and apostles of Jesus Christ.

> **NOTE: A baptized person already possesses supernatural life, but just as natural life is developed and strengthened in a child, so supernatural life needs to be developed and strengthened. That is what the Holy Ghost does in the sacrament of Confirmation: He brings a greater abundance of gifts to the soul.**

211. *What are the gifts of the Holy Ghost?*

The gifts of the Holy Ghost are wisdom, understanding, knowledge, counsel, fortitude, piety, and fear of the Lord.

> NOTE: These gifts are supernatural qualities placed in the soul by the Holy Ghost, to allow the one who is confirmed to understand his duty better (wisdom, understanding, knowledge, and counsel) and to give him more courage to fulfill it (fortitude, piety, fear of the Lord).

212. *Is Confirmation necessary in order to go to heaven?*

No, Confirmation is not necessary in order to go to heaven, but one would be guilty and would deprive himself of many graces if he neglected to receive it.

• 213. *What must one do to receive Confirmation well?*

To receive Confirmation well, one must be in a state of grace and know the principal truths of the Christian religion.

• 214. *Who ordinarily gives the sacrament of Confirmation?*

Bishops ordinarily give the sacrament of Confirmation.

† 215. *How does the Bishop give the sacrament of Confirmation?*

The Bishop gives the sacrament of Confirmation by imposing his hands on those whom he

confirms and by anointing their forehead with Holy Chrism in the form of a cross.

> NOTE: As he anoints the forehead, the Bishop says: "I sign you with the sign of the cross, and I confirm you with the chrism of salvation, in the name of the Father and of the Son and of the Holy Ghost."
>
> The anointing is made on the forehead in the form of a cross to show that the Christian who has been confirmed should never be ashamed of the cross of Jesus Christ.
>
> After this anointing, the Bishop touches the cheek of the one who has been confirmed, saying: "Peace be with you."
>
> At Confirmation, the boys have a sponsor who is a man, and the girls have a sponsor who is a woman: these are the witnesses of the commitment which the newly confirmed person is taking upon himself to live as a Christian.

216. *What is Holy Chrism?*

Holy Chrism is a mixture of olive oil and balm consecrated by the Bishop on Holy Thursday.

> NOTE: The oil symbolizes the sweetness and strength of grace, while the balm symbolizes the virtues which the person who has been confirmed should practice.

Confirmation

> **FOR MY LIFE** – I was signed with the sign of the cross on the day of my Confirmation. I will never blush at being a Christian, nor will I be ashamed of the cross of Jesus Christ.
>
> **PRAYER** – "O my God, grant me to be a true Christian, a complete Christian, an apostle."
>
> **THE WORD OF GOD** – "You shall receive the power of the Holy Ghost coming upon you, and you shall be witnesses unto Me…." (Acts 1:8)

LITURGY – After he has given Confirmation, the Bishop blesses the confirmands and has them recite aloud the "Apostles' Creed", the "Our Father" and the "Hail Mary," the beautiful prayers of a Christian.

ASSIGNMENT – What does the sacrament of Confirmation give us? – Does it give us more than Baptism does? – Have we not already received the Holy Ghost? – What is the great grace of the sacrament of Confirmation? – For what does the sacrament of Confirmation prepare us?

PROJECT – Draw a picture representing the Bishop giving the sacrament of Confirmation, or make a photograph album illustrating the liturgy of the sacrament of Confirmation.

LESSON 33

JESUS CHRIST NOURISHES OUR SUPERNATURAL LIFE

THE EUCHARIST

When you studied the life of Jesus, you admired His power; He can do anything He wants. Lazarus had been dead for several days and his body was already decomposing in the tomb, when Jesus came and said: "Lazarus, come forth." Lazarus arose, full of life.[36]

Jesus wanted to give us His Body as food. After the miracle of the multiplication of the loaves, He promised it to His Apostles and to the Jews who were following Him: "I am the bread of life," He said: "If any man eat of this bread, he shall live forever; and the bread that I will give, is My Flesh…"[37]

On the night before His death, Holy Thursday evening, when He had gathered His Apostles for a last

---

[36] John 11:1-45
[37] John 6: 48-52

THE EUCHARIST

meal, He said to them: "With desire I have desired to eat this Pasch with you…"[38]

During the supper, He took bread and, after giving thanks, He blessed it, broke it, and gave it to His disciples, saying: "Take all of you and eat of this: for this is My Body, which shall be delivered for you." He then took a chalice and, after giving thanks, He gave it to them, saying, "Take all of you and drink of this: for this is the chalice of My Blood, the Blood of the new and eternal covenant which shall be shed for you and for many unto the remission of sins. Do this for a commemoration of Me."

Understand well what Jesus had just done; as soon as He said: "This is My Body," the bread was changed into His Body; as soon as He said, "This is My Blood," the wine was changed into His Blood.

The Eucharist was instituted on that day.[39]

REVIEW – Using an example, show that Jesus can do anything He wills. – What did Jesus promise? – What did Jesus say as He took bread in His hands? as He took the wine? – What happened after He had spoken?

LESSON

† 217. *What is the Eucharist?*

The Eucharist is a sacrament which contains the Body, Blood, Soul, and Divinity of Jesus Christ under the appearances of bread and wine.

---

[38] Luke 22:15
[39] cf. Luke 22; I Cor. 11

- 218. *When did Jesus Christ institute the sacrament of the Eucharist?*

Jesus Christ instituted the sacrament of the Eucharist on Holy Thursday, on the eve of His death.

† 219. *What did Jesus Christ do to institute the Eucharist?*

To institute the Eucharist, Jesus Christ took bread, blessed it, broke it, and gave it to His Apostles, saying: "Take and eat, for this is My Body." He then took the chalice of wine and gave it to His Apostles, saying: "Take and drink, for this is My Blood; do this in memory of Me."

- 220. *What did Jesus do by saying these words: "This is My Body; this is My Blood"?*

By saying these words: "This is My Body; this is My Blood," Jesus Christ changed the bread into His Body and the wine into His Blood.

- 221. *What did Jesus do by saying these words: "Do this in memory of Me"?*

By saying these words, "Do this in memory of Me," Jesus Christ gave to His Apostles and to all priests the power to change bread into His Body and wine into His Blood, as He had done.

- 222. *When does the change of bread and wine into the Body and Blood of Jesus Christ take place?*

The change of bread and wine into the Body and Blood of Jesus Christ takes place at Mass, at the Consecration, when the priest pronounces the very words of Jesus Christ: "This is My Body; This is My Blood."

223. *What is on the altar before the Consecration?*

Before the Consecration, only bread and wine are on the altar.

224. *What is on the altar after the Consecration?*

After the Consecration, Jesus Christ is on the altar, whole and entire under the appearances of bread, and whole and entire under the appearances of wine.

225. *Why did Jesus Christ institute the Eucharist?*

Jesus Christ instituted the Eucharist:
- 1st to continue to offer Himself in sacrifice to God His Father;
- 2nd to be the nourishment of our souls in Communion;
- 3rd to remain always with us.

226. *What are your duties toward Jesus Christ present in the Eucharist?*

My duties toward Jesus Christ present in the Eucharist are:
- 1st to adore Him;
- 2nd to respect the places where He is present;
- 3rd to visit Him in His churches.

> **FOR MY LIFE** – Upon entering the church, I will make my genuflection with faith before the tabernacle covered with the tabernacle veil, where Jesus Christ is present under the appearances of the host.
>
> I will often make a visit to the Blessed Sacrament.
>
> **PRAYER** – "O hidden God, I adore you with all my soul."
>
> **THE WORD OF GOD** – "I am the bread of life: he that cometh to Me shall not hunger: and he that believeth in Me shall never thirst." (John 6:35)

LITURGY – The Church has placed the feast of Our Lord Jesus Christ present in the Eucharist on the Thursday after the Feast of the Holy Trinity. We call this day the Feast of Corpus Christi.

Beautiful processions take place on this occasion.

Every year, Perpetual Adoration takes place in every parish.

ASSIGNMENT – What day recalls the institution of the Holy Eucharist? – Do you know any other feasts in honor of the Holy Eucharist? – What indicates the presence of the Holy Eucharist in the tabernacle? – What should one do before the altar where the Holy Eucharist is present? – What is the name of the sacred vessel used to expose the Holy Eucharist? – How should one make the genuflection before the Holy Eucharist exposed on the altar?

The Eucharist

Project – Construct a table of the Last Supper showing the places of Christ and the Apostles. Make a diptych representing on one side the promise of the Eucharist, on the other side its institution.

LESSON 34

THE HOLY SACRIFICE OF THE MASS

To understand well what the Mass is, reflect on the following table: It is the same Victim and the same prayer of Jesus.

Who is on the cross? Jesus Christ, the Son of God.	The priest has just said: "This is My Body; this is My Blood." *Who is on the altar?*
In what state was Jesus? That of a victim. The Blood flows from His Body through His wounds.	*In what state is Jesus?* That of a victim. The Precious Blood in the chalice and the Body of Christ in the host represent the separation of the Body and the Blood of Jesus, as on Calvary.

What does Jesus do on the cross?	*What does Jesus do on the altar?*
He offers Himself to His Father, saying to Him: "You are the Sovereign Master of all things." I thank You for all that You do for men. Forgive them their sins. Give them Your grace.	He offers Himself to His Father by the hands of the priest and there again He says to His Father that He is the Sovereign Master. He thanks Him for His benefits. He asks forgiveness for sins. He calls down all graces for us.
On the cross, Jesus was visible. On the cross, the sacrifice was bloody. Jesus suffered. Jesus died.	On the altar, Jesus is invisible. On the altar, the sacrifice is unbloody. Jesus risen from the dead can no longer suffer. He can no longer die.

***It is the same Victim and
the same prayer of Jesus.***

Throughout the world, at every hour of the day, the great prayer of the Mass continues without ceasing.

REVIEW – Who is the Victim on the cross? – Who offers Himself by the hands of the priest at Mass? – What did

Jesus pray for on the cross? – What does He pray for on the altar? – What differences do you see between the sacrifice of the cross and the sacrifice of the Mass?

LESSON

227. *What is the Mass?*

The Mass is the sacrifice in which Jesus Christ offers Himself to God His Father, as a victim for us, through the ministry of the priests.

NOTE: A "sacrifice" is the offering or immolation of a victim to God in order to acknowledge that He is the sovereign Master of all things.

Long ago, men offered to God animals which they immolated.

• 228. *Why did Jesus Christ institute the sacrifice of the Mass?*

Jesus Christ instituted the sacrifice of the Mass in order to recall and continue every day the sacrifice of the cross.

229. *How does the sacrifice of the Mass continue the sacrifice of the cross?*

The sacrifice of the Mass continues the sacrifice of the cross because, on the altar as on the cross, it is always the same Priest and the same Victim: Jesus Christ really present, offering Himself in expiation for our sins.

230. *To whom is the sacrifice of the Mass offered?*

The sacrifice of the Mass is offered to God alone, because it is an act of adoration.

231. *Why is the sacrifice of the Mass offered to God?*

The sacrifice of the Mass is offered to God in order to adore Him, thank Him, ask His forgiveness, and obtain His graces.

> NOTE: Although the sacrifice of the Mass can only be offered to God, we can nonetheless offer it to Him in honor of the Blessed Virgin and the Saints, in order to thank God for the graces which He granted them and to obtain their intercession.

232. *For whom does the priest offer the sacrifice of the Mass?*

The priest offers the sacrifice of the Mass for the living and the dead, and in particular for the intentions of those who requested the Mass.

• 233. *What is the best manner of assisting at the holy sacrifice of the Mass?*

The best manner of assisting at the holy sacrifice of the Mass is to follow the prayers of the priest, with the same sentiments which we would have had at the foot of the cross.

234. *What benefit is there in frequently assisting at Mass, even during the week?*

There is a great benefit in frequently assisting at Mass, even during the week, because a true child of God frequently offers his life, his suffer-

ings and his actions in union with the sacrifice of Christ.

> **NOTE:** "I beseech you therefore, brethren, by the mercy of God, that you present your bodies a living sacrifice, holy, pleasing unto God, your reasonable service." (Romans 12:1)

FOR MY LIFE – I will never fail to assist at Mass when the Church asks it and I will unite myself to the Mass with all my soul, because I understand that nothing could be more agreeable to God than the sacrifice of the Mass.

PRAYER – "Grant, O Jesus, that Your sacrifice might also be my sacrifice; and that it may be so, unite my will to Yours."

THE WORD OF GOD – "For as often as you shall eat this bread, and drink the chalice, you shall show the death of the Lord, until He come." (I Cor. 11:26)

LITURGY – The Mass is made up of two main parts: a teaching part, called the Mass of the catechumens, and the sacrifice properly so called, or the Mass of the faithful. The sacrifice itself is made up of three phases, or principal parts: the Offertory, the Consecration and the Communion.

ASSIGNMENT – What sacred vessels are necessary for the Mass? – What linens and sacred vestments are used by the priest to say Mass? – Describe the altar when Mass begins. What are the principal parts of the Mass?

– What dispositions are essential in order to participate well at the holy sacrifice of the Mass?

PROJECT – Construct a miniature altar, taking as a model the high altar of your church. Sew linens and sacred vestments to match this altar. Make a series of friezes illustrating the history of sacrifice in the Old Testament, its promise and its realization in the New Testament.

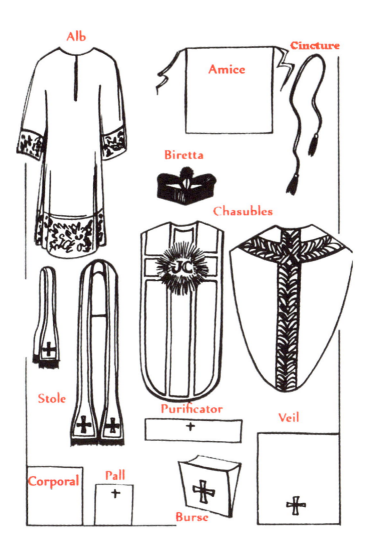

LESSON 35

HOLY COMMUNION

Communion is the most intimate union possible between us and Our Lord. When you receive Communion, you receive Our Lord so truly that you are lost in Him and He in you, and you can say: "It is no longer I who live, it is Jesus Christ who lives in me," for when you have eaten the Body of Our Lord under the species of bread, Jesus truly becomes the nourishment of your soul.

That is exactly what the Master Himself said in speaking of the Eucharist when, after the miracle of the multiplication of the loaves of bread, He promised it to us: "I am the bread of life. This is the bread which cometh down from heaven... If any man eat of this bread, he shall live forever; and the bread that I will give, is My Flesh, for the life of the world."

When He spoke these words, the Jews disputed among themselves, saying: "How can this man give us his flesh to eat?" Jesus said to them: "Amen, amen I say unto you: Except you eat the Flesh of the Son of man, and drink His Blood, you shall not have life in you. He that eateth My Flesh and drinketh My Blood, hath everlasting life: and I will raise him up on the last day. For My Flesh is meat indeed: and My Blood is drink indeed. He that eateth My Flesh, and drinketh My Blood, abideth in Me, and I in him."[40]

Remember this carefully: Communion is the food necessary for your soul.

REVIEW – What can you say when you have received Communion? – At what moment did Jesus say: "I am the bread of life"? – What did the Jews say? – Quote the sentence in which Jesus says that His Flesh is food.

LESSON

† 235. *What is Holy Communion?*

Holy Communion is the receiving of Jesus Christ in the Eucharist.

NOTE: Jesus Christ said: "My Flesh is meat indeed: and My Blood is drink indeed. He that eateth My Flesh, and drinketh My Blood, abideth in Me, and I in him." (John 6:56)

• 236. *When are we obliged to receive Communion?*

We are obliged to receive Communion each year during the Easter time and when we are dangerously ill.

NOTE: Communion given to the sick in danger of death is called "viaticum," that is to say provisions

---

[40] John 6:48-57

for the great journey from earthly life to eternal life.

When you meet a priest who is carrying Communion to a sick person, greet him respectfully and adore Our Lord who is passing by.

● 237. *Is it good to receive Communion often?*

Yes, it is good to receive Communion often, and even every day, provided that we do so with the necessary dispositions.

† 238. *When are children obliged to receive Communion?*

Children are obliged to receive Communion as soon as they begin to have the use of reason and have been sufficiently prepared.

NOTE: Children may receive Communion as often as grown-ups, even every day, if they do so in order to please God and to become better.

239. *What effects does Communion produce in us?*

Communion produces four effects in us:
- **1st it unites us to Our Lord Jesus Christ;**
- **2nd it increases our supernatural life of grace;**
- **3rd it weakens our evil inclinations;**
- **4th it is a promise of eternal life.**

FOR MY LIFE – I will not only receive Communion when I am obliged to by the law of the Church, but as often as possible, in order to fulfill the desire of Our Lord and to have the strength to remain faithful to Him.

PRAYER – Act of desire: "Lord Jesus, come into my heart; become the Master of my soul and reign there in time and in eternity."

THE WORD OF GOD – "Amen, amen I say unto you: Except you eat the Flesh of the Son of man, and drink His Blood, you shall not have life in you." (John 6:54)

LITURGY – It is possible to receive Communion before, during or after Mass, but the Communion which the Church recommends is Communion during Mass, which allows us to unite ourselves to the sacrifice of Our Lord.

ASSIGNMENT – Can we live without eating? – What nourishes the body? – Does not your intelligence also need food? – What is the food of your intelligence? – Does not your supernatural life need food, as well? – What is that food? – Who said so?

PROJECT – Make a little notebook and illustrate it with pictures of little children receiving Communion.

Lesson 36

HOW TO RECEIVE COMMUNION WELL

Since Communion is a divine food, we might compare it to a feast.

Now, when you are invited to a fancy meal with relatives or friends, you put on your best clothes and you take care to try to look your best. When you receive Communion, be sure you are properly disposed. The first condition of all is to be without mortal sin. Your soul should be in a state of grace.

Read this parable which we could apply to Communion:

One day, there was a king celebrating the wedding of his son, and his servants gathered together all those they found on the road so that the wedding hall was filled with guests.

The king entered to see who was at table and when he saw a man who was not clothed in wedding garments, he said to him: "Friend, how camest thou in hither not having on a wedding garment?" Since the man stood there silent, the king ordered his servants to bind him hand and foot and cast him into the outer darkness, where there would be the weeping and the gnashing of teeth.[41]

You understand that the wedding garment is the state of grace; we must go to the divine banquet free from mortal sin. Saint Paul said the same thing to the first Christians when he reminded them:

"He that eateth and drinketh unworthily, eateth and drinketh judgment to himself, not discerning the Body of the Lord."[42]

When you receive Our Lord, always receive Him like Mary, the sister of Lazarus, who poured a perfume of great price on the feet of Jesus. The perfume will be the love you have for Jesus.

REVIEW – To what might we compare Communion? – What do you do when you are invited to a fancy meal? – What is meant by the parable of the marriage feast? – What resolutions can you make?

LESSON

240. *What is necessary to receive Communion well?*

**To receive Communion well it is necessary:
1st to be in a state of grace;
2nd to have an upright intention.**

> NOTE: Having an upright intention means receiving Communion in order to obey Our Lord, unite

---

[41] Matthew 22: 1-14
[42] I Cor. 11:29

oneself to Him, and so become better. We should never receive Communion simply out of habit or out of vanity.

● 241. *What sin would one commit who received Communion in a state of mortal sin?*

One who received Communion in a state of mortal sin would commit a sacrilege, because he would be profaning the Body of Our Lord Jesus Christ.

242. *What else is necessary to receive Communion?*

To receive Communion, it is also necessary to be fasting, that is to say:
Neither to eat nor drink one hour before receiving Communion.
We may drink natural water at any time, or a medicine necessary for our health.

> NOTE: 1. The Church asks us to fast before Communion out of respect for the Body of Christ and in a spirit of penance.
>
> 2. The Church relaxed the law of the Eucharistic fast in order to make frequent Communion possible for the faithful.
>
> 3. The sick, even those who are not bed-ridden, may drink non-alcoholic beverages at any time, as well as any solid or liquid medicine.
>
> 4. In danger of death, one may receive Communion without having fasted.

How to Receive Communion Well

243. *What should you do before Communion?*

Before Communion, I should speak to Our Lord, making acts of faith, of contrition, of love, and of desire.

244. *What should you do after Communion?*

After Communion, I should adore Our Lord, thank Him, ask Him for His graces, and promise Him to live in a more Christian manner.

> FOR MY LIFE – I will only receive Communion when I am sure of having no grave sin on my conscience. When I have venial sins, I will remember that one of the effects of Communion is to take them away, and I will receive this sacrament of love asking Jesus to forgive me for these sins.
>
> PRAYER – "Lord, I am not worthy that You should come into my soul, but only say the word and my soul shall be healed."
>
> THE WORD OF GOD – "But let a man prove himself: and so let him eat of that Bread, and drink of the Chalice. For he that eateth and drinketh unworthily, eateth and drinketh judgment to himself, not discerning the Body of the Lord." (I Cor. 11:28-29)

LITURGY – When the priest gives Communion, he says: "May the Body of Our Lord Jesus Christ preserve your soul unto life everlasting."

When he gives viaticum to those in danger of death, he says: "Receive, brother (or sister), the viaticum of the Body of Our Lord Jesus Christ; may He preserve you from the snares of the enemy and lead you to eternal life."

ASSIGNMENT – May you receive Communion every day? – On what conditions? – If one has committed venial sins, may one receive Communion? – May one receive Communion without having been to Confession? – What should one do after receiving Communion?

PROJECT – Illustrate with two scenes from the Gospel the two conditions necessary to receive Communion well: the state of grace and an upright intention.

Make a clay model or a stage with moveable characters representing the conversation of Our Lord with the Centurion.

LESSON 37

JESUS CHRIST GIVES US BACK OUR SUPERNATURAL LIFE

PENANCE

Jesus, the Son of God, had the power to forgive sins. He showed it clearly by a miracle. One day as Jesus was teaching in a house where there were many people, some men tried to enter, carrying a paralytic on a stretcher. They could not enter on account of the crowd, and so they climbed up onto the terrace, took away a few of the tiles that made the roof, and lowered the paralytic on his stretcher right in front of Jesus. Seeing their faith, Christ said to the paralyzed man: "Son, thy sins are forgiven thee." Some Jews who were there began to think in their hearts: "Why doth this man speak thus? He blasphemeth. Who can forgive sins, but God only?" Jesus said to them: "Why think you these things in your hearts? Which is easier, to say to the sick of the palsy: Thy sins are forgiven thee; or to say: Arise, take up thy bed and walk? But that you may know that the Son of Man hath power on earth to forgive sins," he said to the paralytic, "I say to thee: Arise. Take up thy bed and go into thy house."

At that instant the man stood up in front of them, took the stretcher on which he had been lying, and went back to his house, glorifying God.[43]

Jesus had just proven by a miracle that He had the power to forgive sins. He gave this power to the Apostles and their successors.

On the evening of His resurrection, Jesus appeared to His Apostles who had locked themselves in the Upper Room, and after saying to them twice: "Peace be to you," He added: "As the Father hath sent Me, I also send you." Then He breathed on them, saying: "Receive ye the Holy Ghost. Whose sins you shall forgive, they are forgiven them: and whose sins you shall retain, they are retained."[44]

REVIEW – What did the Jews do, who were carrying the paralytic? – What did Jesus say to that man? – What were some of the Jews thinking? – How did Jesus prove that He had the power to forgive sins? – At what time and in what circumstances did He give that power to His Apostles?

---

[43] Mark 2:1-12
[44] John 20:21-23

LESSON

† 245. *What is Penance?*

Penance is a sacrament which forgives the sins committed after Baptism.

† 246. *When did Jesus Christ institute the sacrament of Penance?*

Jesus Christ instituted the sacrament of Penance on the evening of His resurrection, when He said to His Apostles: "Receive ye the Holy Ghost. Whose sins you shall forgive, they are forgiven them: whose sins you shall retain, they are retained."

247. *Who has the power to forgive sins?*

Those who have the power to forgive sins are the Bishops, successors of the Apostles, and the priests authorized by the Bishops.

• 248. *For whom is the sacrament of Penance obligatory?*

The sacrament of Penance is obligatory for all those who have committed a mortal sin.

† 249. *At what moment do you receive the sacrament of Penance?*

I receive the sacrament of Penance at the moment when the priest gives me absolution.

- 250. *What is absolution?*

Absolution is a judgment which the priest pronounces in the name of Jesus Christ, to forgive sins.

† 251. *What should you do to obtain the pardon of your sins by absolution?*

To obtain the pardon of my sins by absolution, I should:

1st sincerely regret my sins (which is contrition)
2nd tell them to the priest (which is confession)
3rd repair the offense done to God and to my neighbor (which is reparation or satisfaction).

NOTE: 1st Among these three conditions, contrition is the most necessary. Without contrition one can never obtain forgiveness, even of venial sins.

2nd To fulfill the third condition, it is necessary to have the will to make reparation, at the moment of the absolution.

> **FOR MY LIFE** – I will go to Confession regularly. If one day I am afraid of going to Confession, I will remember that Jesus instituted this sacrament out of kindness toward us, and that the priest represents Him.
>
> **PRAYER** – "My God, grant that I may never be afraid of this sacrament of forgiveness."
>
> **THE WORD OF GOD** – "Amen I say to you, whatsoever you shall bind upon earth, shall be bound also in heaven; and whatsoever you shall loose upon earth, shall be loosed also in heaven." (Matthew 18:18)

LITURGY – To give absolution, the priest says to the penitent who has just accused himself of his sins: "I absolve you of your sins in the name of the Father and of the Son and of the Holy Ghost. Amen."

ASSIGNMENT – Your friend Peter says to you: "I have no sins on my soul. I do not need to go to Confession. I will go to Confession when I have committed a mortal sin." Is he right? If not, what would you tell him to prove that he is wrong?

PROJECT – Make a model out of cardboard or wood, with a background representing the institution of the sacrament of Penance, and in the foreground a confessional.

Lesson 38

Contrition

You learned in the preceding lesson that three things are necessary to obtain the pardon of our sins by absolution: to regret them sincerely, to confess them, and to make reparation for them.

Jesus explains these things to us in the parable of the Prodigal Son. You know that a parable is a story made up by Jesus to help us understand His teaching.

A man had two sons. The younger son said to his father: "Father, give me the portion of substance that falleth to me." The father divided his goods. A few days later, the younger son gathered together everything that he owned and went off into a faraway country where he squandered his fortune in riotous living.

When he had spent everything, a great famine came upon the land and he began to experience want.

He therefore went off and placed himself in the service of a citizen of that country, who sent him to his farm to watch over his swine. He would very much

CONTRITION

have liked to satisfy his hunger on what these animals ate, but no one gave him anything. Then, returning to himself, he said: "How many hired servants in my father's house abound with bread, and I here perish with hunger?

"I will arise, and will go to my father, and say to him: 'Father, I have sinned against heaven and before thee. I am not worthy to be called thy son: make me as one of thy hired servants.'"[45]

Before finding out what happens next, you need to understand what the beginning of the story means. The prodigal son had sinned. He looked at his sin as the greatest evil that had ever happened to him. His regret applied to everything he had done wrong and he regretted it because he still loved his father.

You have guessed it: the prodigal son represents the sinner.

REVIEW – What is a parable? – What does the younger son ask of his father? – What does he do with his money? – Why is he obliged to place himself in the service of a farmer? – What happens in his soul? – What resolution does he make? – Who is the prodigal son?

LESSON

† 252. *What does it mean to have contrition?*

To have contrition means sincerely to regret one's sins with the firm resolution not to commit them again.

---

[45] Luke 15:11-19

253. *Why should you have a firm resolution not to sin again in the future?*

I should have the firm resolution not to sin again in the future because without this resolution I would not really regret my sins.

• 254. *How many kinds of contrition are there?*

There are two kinds of contrition: perfect contrition and imperfect contrition.

• 255. *When do you have perfect contrition?*

I have perfect contrition when I regret my sins because sin is an offense against God Who is infinitely good, and because it caused the death of Our Lord.

• 256. *When do you have imperfect contrition?*

I have imperfect contrition when I regret my sins out of shame at having committed them, or out of fear of hell.

257. *What does perfect contrition do?*

Perfect contrition takes away sin even before absolution, provided one has the desire to go to Confession.

258. *What does imperfect contrition do?*

Imperfect contrition does not take away sin, but it disposes us to receive forgiveness for it in the sacrament of Penance.

Contrition

† 259. *Make an act of contrition.*

O my God, I am heartily sorry for having offended Thee, and I detest all my sins because I dread the loss of heaven and the pains of hell; but most of all because they offend Thee, my God, Who art all good and deserving of all my love. I firmly resolve, with the help of Thy grace, to confess my sins, to do penance, and to amend my life. Amen.

NOTE: A good Christian should make an act of perfect contrition:

1st when he has had the misfortune of committing a mortal sin;

2nd if he is in danger of death.

FOR MY LIFE – I will never forget that contrition is primary in the sacrament of Penance; I will always ask God for the grace of contrition before presenting myself to receive it.

PRAYER – "Behold me, Lord, covered in confusion and filled with sorrow at the sight of my sins. I come before Thee to detest them with a true sorrow at having offended a God Who is so good, so loving and so worthy of being loved."

THE WORD OF GOD – "I say to you, that even so there shall be joy in heaven upon one sinner that doth penance, more than upon ninety-nine just who need not penance." (Luke 15:7)

Liturgy – Certain psalms evoke sentiments of regret in terms that are particularly expressive. These psalms are called Penitential Psalms. The best known is the one which begins with the word "Miserere," which means: "Have pity."

Assignment – Your cousin Paul says to you: "I am incapable of having contrition because I know very well that I am going to sin again." What do you think of what he says? If he is wrong, say why.

Project – Make a series of clay models showing the different scenes of the parable of the prodigal son.

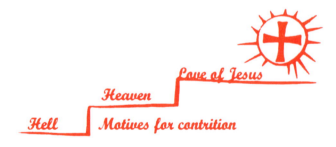

Lesson 39

Confession

You remember what the prodigal son decided after sincerely regretting his sin: "I will arise, and will go to my father, and say to him: Father, I have sinned against heaven, and before thee." He did so. He rose up and went toward his father.

When he was yet a great way off, his father saw him and was moved with compassion, and running to him fell upon his neck and kissed him. His son said to him: "Father, I have sinned against heaven, and before thee: I am not worthy to be called thy son."

And the father said to his servants: "Bring forth quickly the first robe, and put it on him, and put a ring on his hand, and shoes on his feet: and bring hither the fatted calf, and kill it, and let us eat and make merry: because this my son was dead, and is come to life again: was lost, and is found." And they began to make merry.[46]

---

[46] Luke 15:18-24

Let us explain this little parable:

The prodigal son is the sinner. As soon as the sinner sincerely regrets his faults, he has the desire to go find the priest in the confessional. There God awaits him to forgive him, as the father awaits the prodigal son.

The sinner accuses himself of his sins to the priest who has the power to forgive him and he receives the assurance of his forgiveness by the absolution.

Once he has been forgiven he becomes again a true child of God and the angels rejoice, because there is more joy in heaven for one sinner who does penance than for ninety-nine just who have no need of repentance.

REVIEW – What had the prodigal son decided to do? – What did he do? – How did his father welcome his confession? – Explain this little story.

LESSON

† 260. *What does it mean to go to Confession?*

To go to Confession means to tell one's sins to a priest in order to receive absolution.

261. *Who instituted Confession?*

Our Lord Jesus Christ instituted Confession.

† 262. *What sins are you obliged to confess?*

I am obliged to accuse myself of all my mortal sins, telling their number and any circumstances that make them more serious.

- 263. *Are you obliged to confess your venial sins?*

I am not obliged to confess my venial sins, but it is very useful for me to do so.

> NOTE: The absolution which you receive after having confessed your venial sins strengthens supernatural life in you and gives you graces to fight against the habit of sin.

† 264. *If you deliberately hide a mortal sin in Confession, would your other sins be forgiven?*

No, if I deliberately hide a mortal sin in Confession, my other sins would not be forgiven and I would commit a sacrilege.

265. *What should one do who has hidden a mortal sin in Confession?*

One who has hidden a mortal sin in Confession should say so to a confessor and do over again his bad Confessions.

266. *Are mortal sins forgiven which were accidentally forgotten in Confession?*

Yes, mortal sins accidentally forgotten in Confession are forgiven, but it is necessary to accuse oneself of them in one's next Confession.

> **FOR MY LIFE** – I will always be frank and sincere in my Confessions. I will never leave the confessional with a troubled conscience.
>
> **PRAYER** – "I confess to almighty God…"
>
> **THE WORD OF GOD** – "I will arise, and will go to my father, and say to him: Father, I have sinned against heaven, and before thee." (Luke 15:18)

LITURGY – In the liturgy of the Mass, the Church has the priest and then the faithful say that they are sinners, by the recitation of the "Confiteor" at the foot of the altar.

ASSIGNMENT – One of your classmates tells you: "I don't see anywhere in the Gospel that Jesus instituted Confession. The priests invented it." What will you answer?

PROJECT – Illustrate the "I confess to almighty God" with a series of drawings.

LESSON 40

THE MANNER OF GOING TO CONFESSION

The lesson which you are about to study will tell you what you should do before, during and after Confession. To help you remember, follow the little captions under the pictures.

What are these children doing?

Answer after reading Question 267.

This child is going to go to Confession.

How will he accuse himself of his sins?

He is embarrassed about telling some of them.

What will he do?

What is this child doing? What prayer is she reciting? What will she say to the priest after accusing herself of her sins?

Answer after reading Questions 268, 269, 270.

These children have just been to Confession.

What are they doing?

Answer after reading Question 271.

LESSON

267. *What should you do to prepare for Confession?*

To prepare for Confession, I should:
  1st ask for the help of God,
  2nd examine my conscience,
  3rd try to have true contrition.

NOTE: To examine my conscience, I ought to look for the sins I have committed against the commandments of God and of the Church, against the virtues I ought to practice, and against my duty of state.

After examining my conscience, I ought to think about the offense my sins have caused God and the suffering which Jesus Christ endured in order to expiate them.

THE MANNER OF GOING TO CONFESSION

• 268. *What will you do when you are in the confessional?*

When I am in the confessional, I will make the sign of the cross and then I will say:

1st "Bless me, Father, for I have sinned";
2nd I will say how long it has been since my last confession;
3rd I will tell my sins.

NOTE: You should remember that the priest stands in the place of Our Lord Jesus Christ and that he has to keep what you say absolutely secret. You therefore ought to accuse yourself of your sins with humility, openness and simplicity, without useless details.

If you are embarrassed to say certain sins, ask the priest to help you, and answer his questions sincerely.

• 269. *What should you do after accusing yourself of your sins?*

After accusing myself of my sins, I should add: "I am sorry for these and all the sins I may have forgotten."

• 270. *What should you do after telling your sorrow for your sins?*

After telling my sorrow for my sins, I should listen to the advice of the confessor and recite the Act of Contrition while he gives me absolution.

271. *What do you do after your Confession?*

After my Confession, I thank God for granting me forgiveness, I renew my resolution to avoid sin and I say my penance as soon as possible.

> **FOR MY LIFE** – I will make my examination of conscience with careful attention.
>
> **PRAYER** – "Holy Ghost, eternal source of light, dispel the darkness which hides from me the ugliness and the wickedness of sin. Grant me, my God, to conceive so great a horror for sin that I might hate it, if it were possible, as much as You hate it Yourself and that I might fear nothing so much as committing it in the future."
>
> **THE WORD OF GOD** – Jesus said of the Publican: "This man went down into his house justified [because of his humility] rather than the other." (Luke 18:14)

LITURGY – You have certainly noticed that there are two sources of grace in every church, always ready to let it come pouring forth: the baptismal font, where the soul may be washed of original sin, and the confessional, where the soul may be washed of actual sins. These are the symbols of the mercy of the Good God, who is always ready to welcome back sinners.

ASSIGNMENT – James comes out of the confessional and starts to tell you what his confessor said to him; you tell him: "I do not want to listen to you." "But I am allowed to tell you! My confessor is bound to keep the secret, but not me!" What do you answer?

The Manner of Going to Confession

Project – Make a filmstrip representing the different actions of the penitent during the course of the Confession.

Lesson 41

Satisfaction or Reparation

Did you notice a certain sentence in the story of the prodigal son? After thinking back over his sins and despising them, he went to confess everything to his father, knowing he would be forgiven, and yet he says: "Father, make me as one of thy hired servants."

To be treated like a hired servant was, in his eyes, a reparation for the evil he had done.

The sinner, who is always a prodigal son, ought also to make up for the offense done to God by his sins and sometimes the evil they have caused his neighbor.

How so? Firstly through the penance imposed by the confessor, ordinarily a prayer we are given to say. It is what we call the sacramental penance. Recite it as soon as possible, sincerely regretting your sins and also with the resolution not to commit them anymore.

In addition to this prayer, make sacrifices for the forgiveness of your sins and do not go looking far for these sacrifices; they are everything that costs you the most: obedience at home, your schoolwork, your

SATISFACTION OR REPARATION

little troubles, your sufferings, your failures, and the practice of fraternal charity with one or another of your school friends.

You can say this every morning in your prayer: "I offer to You, my God, in payment for my sins, all the work of my day, all my efforts, and all my pains."

Turn to Jesus, the Blessed Virgin and the Saints for help in offering fitting satisfaction to God.

REVIEW – What is meant by these words of the prodigal son: "Make me as one of thy hired servants"? – What should the sinner do? – How can he make reparation? – In addition to the sacramental penance, how can you make reparation? – What sacrifices can you make?

LESSON

I. Satisfaction

† 272. *What does it mean to satisfy for your sins?*

To satisfy for my sins means to repair the offense I have committed against God, or the wrong I have done to my neighbor.

> NOTE: The sacrament of Penance takes away the eternal punishment due to sin, but there often remains some punishment to be endured, either in this life or in purgatory.

273. *How do you repair the offense committed against God by your sins?*

I repair the offense committed against God by my sins in performing the penance imposed by the confessor, in doing voluntary penance, and in gaining indulgences.

274. *Should you repair the wrong done to your neighbor?*

Yes, I should repair the wrong done to my neighbor, in his person, in his honor or in his goods, and I will only be forgiven if I wish to make reparation.

II. Indulgences

● 275. *What does it mean to gain an indulgence?*

To gain an indulgence means to obtain from God a lessening or complete remission of the punishment to be endured for our sins which have already been forgiven.

> NOTE: In order to lessen or completely remit the punishment which must still be endured for our forgiven sins, the Church allows us to benefit from the infinite merits of Jesus Christ and from the merits of the Blessed Virgin and the Saints.

276. *How many kinds of indulgences are there?*

There are two kinds of indulgences: plenary indulgences, which remit all the punishment due to sin, and partial indulgences, which only take away a part of it.

● 277. *What is necessary in order to gain an indulgence?*

To gain an indulgence, it is necessary:
1st to have the intention to do so;
2nd to be in the state of grace;
3rd to fulfill exactly the conditions set down by the Church.

Satisfaction or Reparation

NOTE: One may also gain indulgences for the souls in purgatory.

FOR MY LIFE – I will always do my penance as soon as I come out of the confessional.

PRAYER – "My God, I offer you my work and the pains of my day, in expiation of my sins."

THE WORD OF GOD – "Unless you shall do penance, you shall all likewise perish." (Luke 13:3)

LITURGY – After giving absolution, the priest recites this prayer: "May the Passion of Our Lord Jesus Christ, the merits of the Blessed Virgin Mary and of all the Saints, all the good you have done, and all of your sufferings, work to the remission of your sins, the increase of grace and the reward of eternal life."

ASSIGNMENT – "My confessor gave me a decade of the rosary for my penance," your friend Paul tells you. "He is too easy on me. I will do the Stations of the Cross instead; that will be better." What do you think?

"I am scandalized by your Catholic morality," a little Protestant comes and tells you. "Someone can have committed every crime on earth. He gains a plenary indulgence and everything is forgiven." Is this true?

PROJECT – Make a collection of the most beautiful indulgenced prayers and illustrate it with drawings or engravings.

LESSON 42

JESUS CHRIST COMES TO THE AID OF THE SICK

EXTREME UNCTION

A sacrament welcomes us at our entry into life: Baptism. A final sacrament awaits us when death draws near: Extreme Unction.

Jesus, Who promised His paradise to the good thief dying with Him on Calvary, wants to give the assurance of pardon to all Christians in danger of death. The Christian has sinned by his senses: he has sinned by his hands, by his eyes, by his ears, by his mouth... Through the sacrament of Extreme Unction, the priest is going to write the forgiveness of God on the body of the sick person.

Anointing the sick person with holy oil on the eyes, the ears and the lips, he says: "By this holy unction and His own most gracious mercy, may the Lord pardon thee whatever sin thou has committed by sight..., hearing..., etc." And after the anointing, he says this prayer: "O Lord God, Who said by Thine Apostle

James: 'Is any man sick among you? Let him bring in the priests of the Church and let them pray over him, anointing him with oil in the name of the Lord. And the prayer of faith shall save the sick man. And the Lord shall raise him up: and if he be in sin, they shall be forgiven him': we beseech Thee, our Redeemer, by the grace of the Holy Ghost to cure the ailments of this sick person and to heal his wounds, forgive his sins, drive from him all pains of mind and body, and in Thy mercy restore him to full health within and without, that being cured by the help of Thy mercy he may return to his former duties."

REVIEW – Which is the sacrament reserved for the sick in danger of death? – What did Jesus wish to do in instituting this sacrament? – With what does the priest anoint the sick person? – What did Saint James the Apostle say? – After the anointing, what does the priest ask: 1st for the soul? 2nd for the body of the sick person?

LESSON

† 278. *What is Extreme Unction?*

Extreme Unction is a sacrament which gives comfort to the soul and the body of the sick.

279. *How does Extreme Unction give comfort to the soul of the sick?*

Extreme Unction gives comfort to the soul of the sick by taking away the remains of their sins, by strengthening them against temptations and by helping them to die as Christians.

280. *How does Extreme Unction give comfort to the body of the sick?*

Extreme Unction gives comfort to the body of the sick by lessening their pains and even giving health back to the body if God judges it useful for the salvation of their soul.

• 281. *When is it necessary to receive Extreme Unction?*

It is necessary to receive Extreme Unction as soon as one is seriously ill and not to wait until one has lost consciousness.

• 282. *What are the proper conditions for receiving Extreme Unction?*

In order to receive Extreme Unction one must be in the state of grace, or at least have imperfect contrition if one has not been able to go to Confession.

283. *What must those do who are assisting seriously ill people?*

Those who are assisting seriously ill people ought to encourage them to receive the sacraments, call the priest and facilitate his ministry.

284. *How does the priest give Extreme Unction?*

The priest gives Extreme Unction by anointing the sick person with oil on the eyes, ears, nostrils, hands, and feet, and by asking God to forgive him his sins.

Extreme Unction

NOTE: As he anoints, the priest says: "By this holy unction and His own most gracious mercy, may the Lord pardon thee whatever sin thou hast committed by sight…, hearing…, smell…, taste…, speech…, touch…, the power of walking…"

In the room of the sick person who is going to receive Extreme Unction, one must prepare a small table with a white linen, a little bottle of holy water, a blessed palm, six cotton-balls on a plate, a piece of bread on another plate, and water for the priest to purify his fingers.

As death draws near, the priest or one of the assistants recites the prayers of the dying, very ancient and very moving prayers which exhort the sick person to have confidence and to abandon himself to divine mercy.

FOR MY LIFE – In case of grave danger, I will not wait until the last minute to call the priest, either for myself or for others.

PRAYER – "Lord, give to all those who will appear today before You the grace of a pious reception of the last sacraments."

THE WORD OF GOD – "Is any man sick among you? Let him bring in the priests of the Church." (James 5:14)

LITURGY – Here is part of the prayer which the priest says after the anointing: "O Lord God, drive from this sick man all pains of mind and body and in Thy mercy restore him to full health within and without, that being cured by the help of Thy mercy he may return to his former duties."

ASSIGNMENT – Which sacraments ought one to receive when he is seriously ill? – When the priest is called too late, may he still give these sacraments? – Is it a sin not to call the priest on time? – How many times may one receive Extreme Unction? – What must one prepare when the sick person is about to receive Extreme Unction?

PROJECT – Set up a table and arrange on it the various objects which serve in the administration of the Last Sacraments. Make a triptych representing the three sacraments which are given to the sick.

LESSON 43

JESUS CHRIST CHOOSES PRIESTS FOR HIMSELF

HOLY ORDERS

You know how Jesus formed His Apostles for three years and how He gave them His power when He said to them on Holy Thursday, after instituting the Eucharist: "Do this in memory of Me," and then after His resurrection when He charged them to forgive sins.

Yet Jesus said: "I am with you even to the consummation of the world." The Apostles therefore had to ordain bishops and priests; and so they did. To replace the traitor Judas, here is how they chose Matthias: Peter said to his brethren, the Apostles: "Of these men who have companied with us, all the time that the Lord Jesus came in and went out among us, beginning from the baptism of John, until the day wherein He was taken up from us, one of these must be made a witness with us of His resurrection."

They appointed two: Joseph and Matthias. Praying, they said: "Thou, Lord, Who knowest the hearts of all men, show which of these two Thou hast chosen, to take the place of his ministry and apostleship, from which Judas hath by transgression fallen, that he might go to his own place." They drew lots, and the lot fell upon Matthias, and he was numbered with the eleven Apostles. (Acts 1:21-26)

A little later, the Apostles ordained deacons. The number of disciples was increasing and the care of certain Christian widows left much to be desired. Then the twelve Apostles assembled the multitude of the disciples and said to them: "It is not reasonable that we should leave the word of God and serve tables. Wherefore, brethren, look ye out among you seven men of good reputation, full of the Holy Ghost and wisdom, whom we may appoint over this business. But we will give ourselves continually to prayer and to the ministry of the word." (Acts 6:1-4)

In the lesson you are going to study, you will learn how the Bishops, successors of the Apostles, ordain priests today.

REVIEW – On what occasions did Jesus give power to His Apostles? – What did the Apostles do to replace the traitor Judas? – Why did they ordain deacons? – Name one of the deacons chosen.

LESSON

† 285. *What is Holy Orders?*

Holy Orders is a sacrament which consecrates priests and gives them the power and the grace to fulfill their functions in a holy manner.

• 286. *What are the principal functions of the priest?*

The principal functions of the priests are: to say Mass, to give the sacraments and to teach the Christian religion.

• 287. *Who gives the sacrament of Holy Orders?*

Bishops alone give the sacrament of Holy Orders.

288. *Is it a great grace and a great honor to become a priest?*

Yes, it is a great grace and a great honor to become a priest, for the priest stands in the place of Jesus Christ and works as He did for the glory of God and the salvation of souls.

289. *What must one do to receive worthily the sacrament of Holy Orders?*

To receive worthily the sacrament of Holy Orders, one must have a vocation, that is to say, one must be called by God.

290. *How does one know that he is called by God to be a priest?*

One knows that he is called by God to be a priest:

1st When he possesses the necessary knowledge and virtue;
2nd When he has the supernatural desire to be a priest;
3rd When one has been accepted by his Bishop.

NOTE: The child who believes he is called to become a priest ought to speak to his confessor, pray, work a great deal, and lead a very pure life.

The honor which God does to a child in calling him to the priesthood reflects back on his parents. They therefore ought to thank God and, far from opposing themselves to his vocation, they should respect it and help their child to answer.

A man becomes a priest in passing through seven steps: Four minor orders: porter, lector, exorcist, acolyte. Three major orders: subdeacon, deacon, priest.

> FOR MY LIFE – I will see in the priest the representative of Christ and I will have the greatest respect for him. Boys will love to serve Mass as often as they can, for the Church does them honor in letting them fulfill the role of an acolyte.
>
> PRAYER – "Lord, grant us priests, grant us holy priests, and make us docile to their teaching."
>
> THE WORD OF GOD – "The harvest indeed is great, but the labourers are few. Pray ye therefore the Lord of the harvest, that He send labourers into His harvest." (Luke 10:2)

HOLY ORDERS

LITURGY – The ceremonies of priestly ordination, which normally take place on Ember Saturday, are principally composed of the imposition of the hands; then, with the oil of the catechumens, the consecration of the fingers that will touch the Blessed Host; and finally the transmission of the power to forgive sins.

ASSIGNMENT – Where do priests receive their formation? – Is it a beautiful thing to be a priest? – Why should we respect them? – Can we help them? – How? – Why can we not allow women to serve Mass?

PROJECT – Draw a picture representing the various degrees of the sacrament of Holy Orders, or a scene with moveable characters representing the calling of the Apostles.

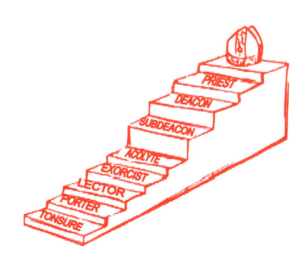

LESSON 44

JESUS CHRIST SANCTIFIES THE FAMILY

I. MATRIMONY

You remember that after creating Adam, God set him in a place called the earthly Paradise. Then he formed the first woman from the body of the man and gave her to Adam as a companion. He thereby established the first human family, performed the first marriage, the model of all other marriages.

The children of Adam and Eve multiplied. The earth was peopled and for a certain time men were faithful to the law willed by God, that only one man be united to only one woman until death. Later on, this law was broken, and in many countries, woman, man's companion, came to be considered as his slave.

Divorce was introduced and permitted. One day as Jesus was teaching the crowds, His enemies approached and tried to trap Him by asking: "Is it lawful for a man to put away his wife for every cause?" Jesus answered them: "Have ye not read, that He

I. Matrimony

who made man from the beginning, made them male and female?" And He said: "For this cause shall a man leave father and mother and cleave to his wife, and they two shall be in one flesh. Therefore now they are not two, but one flesh. What therefore God hath joined together, let no man put asunder."[47]

REVIEW – How did God give a companion to Adam? – What is the great law of marriage willed by God? – What did the Jews ask Jesus about marriage? – What did Jesus reply?

LESSON

† 291. *What is Matrimony?*

Matrimony is a sacrament which unites a man and a woman before God in order to found a Christian family.

NOTE: It is God Who established marriage at the beginning of the world when He created and united Adam and Eve, our first parents.

292. *Who instituted Marriage?*

God instituted Marriage; Jesus Christ elevated it to the level of a sacrament.

293. *Why did Jesus Christ make Marriage a sacrament?*

Jesus Christ made Marriage a sacrament in order to give to Christian spouses the graces necessary to live in a holy manner and to raise their children well.

---

[47] Matthew 19:3-6

> **FOR MY LIFE** – I will have the greatest gratitude toward my parents, who along with God gave me life, the most beautiful gift.
>
> **PRAYER** – "Dear God, bless my parents."
>
> **THE WORD OF GOD** – "What God hath joined together, let no man put asunder." (Matthew 19:6)

LITURGY – The nuptial blessing given during the Wedding Mass reminds us that it is God Who was the author of the union between man and woman, at the beginning of the world: "...O God, by Whom woman is joined to man, and the partnership, ordained from the beginning, is endowed with such blessing that it alone was not withdrawn either by the punishment of original sin, or by the sentence of the flood..."

ASSIGNMENT – You were present at a conversation about your cousin's wedding. Your aunt is not very happy about it. To convince her to accept, your uncle tells her: "After all, if they do not get along they can get a divorce." Is that allowed? Why not?

PROJECT – Make a diorama of the wedding feast of Cana.

LESSON 45

II. THE CONDITIONS OF MATRIMONY

Read your lesson very attentively and explain these points:

There are promises of marriage between...

Why would people post or announce marriages?

Can there be impediments?

What should those people do who know of impediments?

How did these spouses prepare themselves for Matrimony?

If they were not in a state of grace, would they still be married?

Who is the priest? Who are the people beside the spouses?

You will find the answers to these questions in the numbers and notes of the lesson.

LESSON

† 294. *What are the ends of Matrimony?*

To live as Christians, the spouses must be faithful to the ends of Matrimony:

   1st to have children and to raise them as Christians;
   2nd to love one another and to stay faithful to each other.

• 295. *Would spouses who refused to have children commit a grave sin?*

Yes, spouses who refused to have children would commit a grave sin.

• 296. *Can marriage be ended by divorce?*

No, marriage cannot under any circumstances be ended by divorce, even if the other spouse is at fault. Only the death of one of the spouses permits the other to remarry.

297. *May a person remarry who, even without fault of his own, is separated from her husband or from his wife?*

No, a person who is separated from her husband or from his wife may not remarry. That person's only legitimate spouse before God remains the one to whom he was joined in the sacrament of Matrimony. That person may, however, re-

II. The Conditions of Matrimony

ceive the sacraments after asking counsel from a priest.

● 298. *What is necessary for the Marriage of Catholics to be valid?*

For the Marriage of Catholics to be valid, it is necessary that:

> 1st no impediment render the Marriage null;
> 2nd the fiancés freely exchange their consent;
> 3rd the Marriage be celebrated before the parish priest or his delegate, and before two witnesses.
>
> NOTE: The principal impediments to Matrimony are: close blood relation, grave constraint eliminating free choice, previous engagements, and difference of religion.
>
> For the parish priest to know whether impediments exist, it is necessary to make inquiries and publish the banns of the future spouses, that is to announce or post the future marriage. Those who know of impediments are obliged to make them known as soon as possible.

● 299. *Are those Catholics who go to be married before a justice of the peace truly married?*

No, Catholics who go before a justice of the peace to be married are not truly married.

299b. *Does a person put his soul at risk who marries someone of a different religion?*

Yes, a person who marries someone of a different religion would be putting his soul gravely at

risk. He is in danger of not remaining Catholic and of losing eternal life.

300. *How is it necessary to prepare for the sacrament of Matrimony?*

It is necessary to prepare for the sacrament of Matrimony by prayer, an exemplary conduct, and a good confession. The fiancés do not have the right to live together.

> NOTE: Those who receive the sacrament of Matrimony without being in a state of grace are really married, but they commit a sacrilege.

III. THE RELIGIOUS VOCATION

301. *Are all Christians called to marry?*

No, not all Christians are called to marry. God calls some of them to a more perfect life: to be priests or religious.

• 302. *What should a person do who believes he is called to the religious life?*

A person who believes he is called to the religious life should pray, take counsel, and reply generously to the call of God.

> NOTE: Religious offer themselves totally to God by making three vows: Poverty, Chastity, Obedience.

II. THE CONDITIONS OF MATRIMONY

> **FOR MY LIFE** – I will be faithful to my vocation, whatever it may be and whatever sacrifice it may impose.
>
> **PRAYER** – "O my God, make me know Your will for me and give me the courage to fulfill it."
>
> **THE WORD OF GOD** – "Marriage honorable in all." (Hebrews 13:4)

LITURGY – The parish priest or his delegate comes before the spouses who await him at the entrance of the sanctuary.

The spouses answer the questions of the celebrant and exchange their mutual consent. Next they give one another their right hand and the priest blesses them, saying: "I unite you in holy Matrimony in the name of the Father and of the Son and of the Holy Ghost. Amen." Then he sprinkles them with holy water. Next he blesses the ring of the bride.

During the Wedding Mass, the priest gives the nuptial blessing after the Pater Noster.

ASSIGNMENT – May a person marry just anyone? – May a person marry just anywhere? – Before whom should the marriage be celebrated? – May just anyone be a priest or a religious? – What is necessary? – Of whom should one ask advice to know what decision to make?

PROJECT – Make a construction representing the Holy Family at Nazareth.

THIRD PART

The Commandments Which Jesus Christ Gave to Us

JESUS CHRIST SAID: "I AM…**THE WAY**."

*Jesus Christ is our model:
let us imitate Him
"I have given you an example that as I have done,
so you do also." (John 13:15)*

LESSON 46

THE IMITATION OF OUR LORD JESUS CHRIST

THE COMMANDMENTS

One day as Jesus was setting out on a journey, a young man ran up to Him and said: "Good Master, what good shall I do that I may have life everlasting?" Jesus answered him: "Keep the commandments." The man said to Jesus: "Which?" And Jesus reminded him of the commandments that God gave to Moses on Mount Sinai (the same ones you will study in the lesson).

The young man said to him: "All these I have kept from my youth. What is yet wanting to me?" – "If thou wilt be perfect, go sell what thou hast, and give to the poor, and thou shalt have treasure in heaven." But the young man was rich and did not have the courage to follow the counsel of Jesus.[48]

Understand well Jesus' answer. He says to us: "Keep the commandments... Do not think that I am come to destroy the law, or the prophets. I am not come to destroy, but to fulfill."

It was in the Sermon on the Mount that Jesus showed all the beauty of His moral teaching. His words begin with the Beatitudes:

"Blessed are the poor in spirit: for theirs is the kingdom of heaven.

"Blessed are the meek: for they shall possess the land.

"Blessed are they that mourn: for they shall be comforted.

"Blessed are they that hunger and thirst after justice: for they shall have their fill.

"Blessed are the merciful: for they shall obtain mercy.

"Blessed are the clean of heart: for they shall see God. "Blessed are the peacemakers: for they shall be called the children of God.

"Blessed are they that suffer persecution for justice's sake: for theirs is the kingdom of heaven." (Matthew 5)

REVIEW – Use the story to show that Jesus did not come to abolish the commandments. – Read the Beati-

---

[48] Matthew 19:16-22

tudes. Which are the two that you like the best? Tell why.

LESSON

† 303. *Who is the great model of all Christians?*

The great model of all Christians is Our Lord Jesus Christ Himself, for He said to His disciples: "I have given you an example, that as I have done to you, so you do also."[49]

• 304. *What should you do to imitate Our Lord Jesus Christ?*

To imitate Our Lord Jesus Christ, I ought always to do the will of God, our Father, as Jesus Himself, Who said: "I do always the things that please the Father."[50]

305. *How do you firstly know the will of God?*

I know the will of God firstly by the Ten Commandments which God gave to Moses on Mount Sinai: they are called the Mosaic Law, or the law of fear.

† 306. *Recite the commandments of God.*

1. **I am the Lord thy God, thou shalt not have strange gods before Me.**

2. **Thou shalt not take the name of the Lord thy God in vain.**

---

[49] John 13:15
[50] John 8:29

3. Remember thou keep holy the Lord's day.

4. Honor thy father and thy mother.

5. Thou shalt not kill.

6. Thou shalt not commit adultery.

7. Thou shalt not steal.

8. Thou shalt not bear false witness against thy neighbor.

9. Thou shalt not covet thy neighbor's wife.

10. Thou shalt not covet thy neighbor's goods.

307. *How do you know above all the will of God?*

I know the will of God above all by the teaching of Our Lord in His Gospel: it is called the Law of the Gospel, or the law of love.

† 308. *Where did Jesus give to us His law of love?*

Jesus gave to us His law of love especially in the Sermon on the Mount.

> NOTE: It was in the Sermon on the Mount that Our Lord presented His moral code, which is so beautiful and so perfect.
>
> This discourse begins with the Beatitudes. You will find them in the Gospel for the Feast of All Saints.

† 309. *What is the great commandment by which Jesus Christ summarized His entire law of love?*

The great commandment by which Jesus Christ summarized His entire law of love is the commandment of charity: "Thou shalt love the Lord

THE COMMANDMENTS

thy God with thy whole heart and with thy whole soul and with all thy strength and with all thy mind: and thy neighbour as thyself."[51]

> **FOR MY LIFE** – God not only gave me an interior guide, which is my conscience. He also gave me an exterior guide, which are the commandments. I will be grateful to Him for having thus lighted the path which leads to happiness.
>
> **PRAYER** – "Grant me, my God, to keep Your commandments, in order to dwell in Your love."
>
> **THE WORD OF GOD** – "If you love Me, keep My commandments." (John 14:15)

---

[51] Luke 10:27; cf. Matthew 22:37-40; Mark 12:30-31

This is My beloved Son
HEAR HIM

LITURGY – You read the Beatitudes every year in the Gospel of the Feast of All Saints.

ASSIGNMENT – Under what circumstances were the commandments given to man by God? – What did Our Lord say of these commandments? – Where and how did He complete them?

PROJECT – Make a stained-glass window representing the tables of the Law. Make two friezes, one illustrating the scene on Mount Sinai, the other the Sermon on the Mount.

Lesson 47

The Imitation of Our Lord Jesus Christ

The Virtues

When the sun enters into a house, it comes with its light and its heat, and there is something joyful all around, thanks to its rays.

God is the sunlight of the soul – its life. When you received Baptism as a tiny baby, God entered into your soul like a ray of sunshine into a room and He transformed everything in you. There were good natural dispositions in your soul and God perfected them and gave you the means to perform supernatural acts, meritorious for heaven.

He gave you three beautiful virtues which bind you to Him like three cords: Faith, Hope, and Charity.

Along with these theological virtues, we also have the beautiful moral virtues which ought to be the hallmark of a true disciple of Jesus.

When a gardener plants seeds in the earth, he labors the soil so that those seeds might not perish but sprout and develop. Do you want the divine seeds of virtues to stay in your soul and grow? Pray, receive the sacraments, and often make acts of faith, hope and love of God. Do not be afraid to suffer in order to be virtuous. In his Epistle to the Galatians, Saint Paul wrote: "They that are Christ's have crucified their flesh, with their vices and concupiscences."[52]

Jesus taught this to us when He said: "Enter ye in at the narrow gate: for wide is the gate, and broad is the way that leads to perdition."[53]

"If any man will come after Me, let him deny himself, and take up his cross, and follow Me."(Matthew 16:24)

REVIEW – What do you notice when a ray of sunlight comes into a house? – What did God place in your soul at Baptism? – How does a seed develop? – How do you develop the virtues placed in your soul? – What did Saint Paul say? – What did Jesus say?

LESSON

310. *Which virtues allow us to imitate Our Lord Jesus Christ?*

The virtues that allow us to imitate Our Lord Jesus Christ are the supernatural virtues.

---

[52] Galatians 5:24
[53] Matthew 7:13

The Virtues

- 311. *What is a virtue?*

A virtue is an inclination to will the good and always to do what is pleasing to God.

312. *What is a supernatural virtue?*

A supernatural virtue is a virtue which God gives to us with supernatural life.

- 313. *How many kinds of supernatural virtues are there?*

There are two kinds of supernatural virtues: the theological virtues and the moral virtues.

† 314. *What are the theological virtues?*

The theological virtues are: Faith, Hope and Charity.

> NOTE: These virtues are called theological, because they help us to serve God Himself (theological means: "having to do with God").

- 315. *What are the principal moral virtues?*

The principal moral virtues are: prudence, justice, fortitude, and temperance.

> NOTE: These virtues are called moral because they help us to direct our life well, that is, to have a "moral" life.
>
> Prudence makes us choose the best means to save our soul.
>
> Justice makes us render to each his due.
>
> Fortitude makes us overcome the obstacles that are contrary to our duty.

Temperance teaches us how to moderate properly the pleasures of the senses.

316. *Are there other Christian moral virtues to practice?*

Yes, there are many other Christian moral virtues to practice, in particular humility, kindness, generosity, chastity, sobriety, and mortification.

> NOTE: There are also "natural" virtues. Those who are not baptized or who are not in a state of grace can be good, honest, just, courageous… These "natural" virtues are not enough to merit heaven. However, God takes them into account in giving us graces of conversion.

FOR MY LIFE – So that I may become a true Christian, God not only gave me guides (Jesus, the Blessed Virgin and the Saints); at Baptism He gave me interior powers, which are supernatural virtues, thanks to the merits of Jesus' sacrifice. I will often think of the goodness of God which not only made me in His image by giving me a soul with natural virtues, but also gave me a divine life, to allow me to draw nearer to His perfections.

PRAYER – "O God, grant that I may never forget that I am Your child, in order to have the courage to walk in the footsteps of Your beloved Son, Our Lord Jesus Christ."

THE WORD OF GOD – "Every tree that bringeth not forth good fruit, shall be cut down, and shall be cast into the fire." (Matthew 7:19)

The Virtues

Every tree that brings forth no fruit will be cut down and thrown into the fire.

LITURGY – When you visit churches and especially cathedrals, you will notice that artists represented the Christian virtues in sculptures or paintings.

ASSIGNMENT – Which is the virtue that summarizes all the others? – Why did Jesus say that practicing it is a "new commandment"? – Did Jesus show us how to practice this virtue? In what circumstances? – Do you know other virtues practiced by Jesus?

PROJECT – Illustrate each one of the theological and moral virtues with a scene from the Gospel, using a model, a diorama, or a shadow theater.

Lesson 48

The Theological Virtues

I. The Virtue of Faith

In the Gospel, there is a beautiful example of faith. One day when Jesus had withdrawn into the region of Tyre and Sidon, a Canaanite woman came toward Him and cried out with all her strength: "Have mercy on me, O Lord, Thou Son of David: my daughter is grievously troubled by a devil." Jesus merely kept silent and His disciples said to Him: "Send her away, for she crieth after us."

All of a sudden the woman fell down and adored Him and said: "Lord, help me." Jesus wanted to test her and so He answered: "It is not good to take the bread of the children, and to cast it to the dogs." But she said: "Yea, Lord; for the whelps also eat of the crumbs that fall from the table of their masters." Hearing her, Jesus exclaimed:

I. THE VIRTUE OF FAITH

"O woman, great is thy faith: be it done to thee as thou wilt." And her daughter was cured from that hour.[54]

You see what faith can do. Develop this virtue in your soul, and do not pay any attention if people all around you are doubting Jesus; but always repeat, with Saint Peter: "Thou art Christ, the Son of the living God." Remember that "He that believeth not shall be condemned."[55]

REVIEW – What did the pagan woman want? – What did Jesus answer? – Why did He cure her daughter? – What words of Saint Peter should you say over again to Jesus?

LESSON

- 317. *What is faith?*

Faith is a supernatural virtue by which we believe firmly all the truths which Jesus Christ has revealed to us and which He teaches through His Church.

318. *Is it reasonable to believe the truths revealed by Jesus Christ?*

Yes, it is reasonable to believe the truths revealed by Jesus Christ, because the prophecies and miracles of Our Lord are the very certain proof that He spoke truly.

---

[54] Matthew 15:22-28
[55] Mark 16:16

NOTE: Jesus said to the Jews: "If I do not the works of My Father, believe Me not. But if I do, though you will not believe Me, believe the works." (John 10:37)

- 319. *When would you sin against faith?*

I would sin against faith:

   1st if I willfully doubted a revealed truth;
   2nd if I were ashamed of appearing to be a Christian;
   3rd if I put myself in danger of losing the faith.

NOTE: It is never permitted to deny one's faith or to do or say anything contrary to the faith, even to escape death.

- 320. *How would you put yourself in danger of losing the faith?*

I would put myself in danger of losing the faith:

   1st if I neglected to instruct myself in Christian doctrine;
   2nd if I listened to those who attack it;
   3rd if I read bad books.

NOTE: Your duties toward the faith are: 1st to strengthen it in yourself by prayer and study; 2nd to make it known and loved around you; 3rd to defend it if it is attacked.

- 321. *Make an act of faith.*

O my God, I firmly believe that Thou art one God in three divine Persons, the Father, the Son, and the Holy Ghost; I believe that Thy divine Son became Man, and died for our sins, and that

I. THE VIRTUE OF FAITH

He will come to judge the living and the dead. I believe these and all the truths which the holy Catholic Church teaches, because Thou hast revealed them, Who canst neither deceive nor be deceived.

> FOR MY LIFE – When I say "I believe," I know in Whom I am trusting: ultimately it is Jesus, Truth itself; Jesus, Whose life and doctrine the Church has taught me; Jesus, my Savior and my God.
>
> PRAYER – Act of Faith.
>
> THE WORD OF GOD – "Now this is eternal life: that they may know Thee, the only true God, and Jesus Christ, Whom Thou hast sent." (John 17:3)

LITURGY – In the collect of the Mass of the thirteenth Sunday after Pentecost, we ask God for an increase in faith, hope and charity, that is to say, in the three theological virtues which the grace of God gives to us at Baptism.

ASSIGNMENT – Why do we believe what we cannot fully understand? – Is it reasonable to do so? – Did Jesus show us in the Gospel that He loves it when we believe in Him? – Did He reward faith by miracles? – Do you know any? – Can one be saved when one does not believe in Jesus Christ?

PROJECT – Design a leaflet with drawings representing the miracles worked by Our Lord as a reward for faith.

Lesson 49

The Theological Virtues (Continued)

II. The Virtue of Hope

When you say in your prayer: "Our Father, Who art in heaven," it is as if you were saying to God: "As a child trusts in his father, so I trust in You."

It is God Himself who placed this virtue of hope in your soul on the day of your Baptism. Hope, then, that your heavenly Father will give to you His heaven and the means to reach it. You see how generous He is: Jesus, His divine Son, was going to die on the cross; two thieves were crucified beside Him. One of the two looked at Jesus and, regretting his past life, said to Him: "Lord, remember me when Thou shalt come into Thy kingdom." And Jesus said to him: "This day thou shalt be with Me in paradise."[56]

---

[56] Luke 23:39-43

II. The Virtue of Hope

However, do not have a foolish confidence in your own strength. Do not fall into the sin of presumption. You know how Saint Peter presumed too much on his own strength. He said to Jesus Who was foretelling that all of His Apostles would abandon Him: "Although all shall be scandalized in Thee, yet not I." Alas! At the voice of a maidservant, he was afraid and he said of Jesus: "I know not this man of whom you speak."[57] He wept all his life over this sin, even after Jesus forgave him.

Indeed, Jesus forgives all sins. If Judas had wished, he, too, would have obtained forgiveness from the goodness of God. His first sin was a betrayal. His second was a sin of despair. He went and hanged himself.

Who could despair, when he thinks about Jesus suffering and dying on the cross for our sins?

REVIEW – What confidence ought you to have in God? – Give an example of hope. – Give an example of the sin of presumption. – Give an example of the sin of despair.

LESSON

- 322. *What is hope?*

Hope is a supernatural virtue by which we expect from God, with firm confidence, His grace in this world and eternal happiness in the next.

---

[57] Mark 14:29, 71

323. *Why do we expect from God His grace in this world and eternal happiness in the next?*

We expect from God His grace in this world and eternal happiness in the next because God promised them to us and Jesus Christ merited them.

• 324. *How would you sin against hope?*

I would sin against hope by presumption or by despair.

> NOTE: 1st One sins by presumption when he relies on his own strength to do good and avoid evil, and when he places himself in an occasion of sin.
>
> 2nd One sins by despair when he loses confidence in the goodness of God and when he believes he will not be able to go to heaven.

† 325. *Make an act of hope.*

O my God, relying on Thy infinite goodness and promises, I hope to obtain pardon of my sins, the help of Thy grace, and life everlasting, through the merits of Jesus Christ, my Lord and Redeemer.

FOR MY LIFE – Jesus, who forgave Saint Peter, would have forgiven Judas, if he had not despaired. Whatever my sins, I will never despair of the forgiveness of God.

PRAYERS – Act of Hope.

THE WORD OF GOD – "All things are possible with God." (Mark 10:27)

II. THE VIRTUE OF HOPE

LITURGY – The Jews awaited the coming of the Messiah for many centuries. God renewed the promise of a Savior many times over that period. Throughout the season of Advent, the Church recalls the great hope which consoled humanity during its long wait.

She seeks to awaken in our hearts the same sentiments of hope in Jesus for the salvation of souls. In the Gradual of Ember Wednesday in Advent, She has us sing: "The Lord is nigh unto all them that call upon Him, to all that call upon Him in truth."

ASSIGNMENT – Do you know of Apostles who sinned against hope? – What sins had they committed? – Which of the two sins had the more serious consequences? – Why did Jesus forgive the other sin?

PROJECT – Make a triptych showing the confidence of the Good Thief, the despair of Judas, and the presumption of Saint Peter.

LESSON 50

THE THEOLOGICAL VIRTUES (CONTINUED)

III. THE VIRTUE OF CHARITY

A. The Love of God

One day, a doctor of the law came up to Jesus and asked Him this question: "Master, which is the greatest commandment in the Law?" Jesus said to him: "Thou shalt love the Lord thy God with thy whole heart and with thy whole soul and with thy whole mind. This is the greatest and the first commandment. And the second is like to this: Thou shalt love

CHARITY: THE LOVE OF GOD

thy neighbor as thyself. On these two commandments dependeth the whole Law and the Prophets."[58]

Reflect for a moment and ask yourself why we must love God above all things.

An Apostle explained to the first Christians that they were of the household of the good God and he said to them:

"You are no more strangers and foreigners: but you are fellow citizens with the saints and the domestics of God."[59]

Jesus had expressed this idea in a way that was even more exact. He had told us to speak to God by saying: "Our Father, Who art in heaven." There we have the real reason.

God is our Father; to us and to all men He gave life, a soul with a mind and a will, and all of our senses.

It is for us that He makes the harvest ripen, the sun shine its light, the rain fall. He loves us the way the Good Shepherd loves His sheep, the way the father of the prodigal child loved his son. He loves us to the point of sacrificing His Son Our Lord Jesus Christ, Who died on the cross to save us.

REVIEW – What question did the doctor of the law ask Jesus? – What answer did he receive? – Why should you love God? – What has God done for us?

---

[58] Matthew 22:35-40
[59] Ephesians 2:19

LESSON _____

- 326. *What is charity?*

Charity is a supernatural virtue by which we love God above all things and our neighbor as ourself for the love of God.

> NOTE: Our Lord said that we show that we love God by keeping His commandments: "He that hath My commandments and keepeth them; he it is that loveth Me." (Saint John 14:21)

† 327. *Why must we love God?*

We must love God because He is our infinitely good Father and because He is the Good God.

- 328. *How would you sin against the love of God?*

I would sin against the love of God if I were indifferent toward God or if I committed a mortal sin.

† 329. *Make an act of charity.*

O my God, I love Thee above all things, with my whole heart and soul, because Thou art all good and worthy of all love. I love my neighbor as myself for love of Thee. I forgive all who have injured me and ask pardon of all whom I have injured.

Charity: The Love of God

For my life – The proof of my love of God is firstly, in the effort I make to avoid sin, secondly, in my docility to listen to His interior suggestions and the directives of the Church.

Prayer – Act of Charity: O my God, I love Thee above all things, with my whole heart and soul, because Thou art all good and worthy of all love.

The Word of God – "Thou shalt love the Lord thy God with thy whole heart and with thy whole soul and with thy whole mind. This is the greatest and the first commandment." (Matthew 22:37)

Liturgy – The Gospel for the seventeenth Sunday after Pentecost reminds us that we must love the Lord our God with all our heart, with all our soul and with all our mind, and our neighbor as ourself.

Assignment – Does God deserve to be loved above all things? Why? – What best proves to God that we love Him? – Who are they who have succeeded in loving God as He deserves to be loved?

Project – Make a series of drawings representing the various forms of charity toward God in the history of the Church, since the triple act of charity which Jesus asked of Peter in order to take away his triple denial.

LESSON 51

THE THEOLOGICAL VIRTUES (CONTINUED)

III. THE VIRTUE OF CHARITY

B. The Love of Neighbor

"Thou shalt love thy neighbor as thyself."

If all men can pray to God by saying: "Our Father, Who art in heaven," it is because we are all His children. Therefore we are all brothers, and we should love one another as children of the same big family.

"A new commandment I give unto you: That you love one another, as I have loved you, that you also love one another. By this shall all men know that you are My disciples, if you have love one for another."[60]

---

[60] John 13:34-35

Charity: The Love of Neighbor

The Jews did not like the Samaritans. In the parable of the Good Samaritan, Christ reminds us that there should be no exceptions in our charity.

A certain man went down from Jerusalem to Jericho and fell among robbers, who also stripped him and having wounded him went away, leaving him half dead. And it chanced, that a certain Jewish priest went down the same way: and seeing him, passed by. In like manner, a Levite, when he was near the place and saw him, passed by.

But a certain Samaritan, being on his journey, came near him; and seeing him, was moved with compassion: and going up to him, bound up his wounds, pouring in oil and wine: and setting him upon his own beast, brought him to an inn and took care of him.

The next day, he took out two pence and gave them to the host and said: "Take care of him; and whatsoever thou shalt spend over and above, I, at my return, will repay thee."[61]

You understand what the parable means. Now here is the double rule given by Jesus: "All things whatsoever you would that men should do to you, do you also to them."[62]

REVIEW – What do we conclude from the phrase: "Our Father, Who art in heaven"? – Tell the parable of the Good Samaritan. What does it mean? – What rule did Jesus give?

---

[61] Luke 10:30-35
[62] Matthew 7:12

L̲ESSON̲

- 330. *Can you love God if you do not love your neighbor?*

No, I cannot love God if I do not love my neighbor, and the Apostle John said: "If any man say: 'I love God,' and hateth his brother; he is a liar."[63]

† 331. *Who is your neighbor?*

My neighbor is every man, even my enemies.

332. *Why should you love all men?*

I should love all men because Jesus Christ commanded me to do so and because all men are my brothers, created like me in the image of God and redeemed by the Blood of Jesus Christ.

> NOTE: Jesus said: "Love one another, as I have loved you." (John 15:12)

333. *Why should you love even your enemies?*

I should love even my enemies because Jesus Christ commanded me to do so and because He gave me the example.

> NOTE: "Love your enemies: do good to them that hate you: and pray for them that persecute and calumniate you." (Matthew 5:44)

---

[63] I John 4:20

CHARITY: THE LOVE OF NEIGHBOR

- **334.** *What does it mean to love your neighbor as yourself?*

To love my neighbor as myself means to wish him well and to procure for him the same goods, as far as possible, as I desire for myself.

> NOTE: "All things whatsoever you would that men should do to you, do you also to them." (Matthew 7:12)

335. *What does charity toward your neighbor oblige you to do?*

Charity toward my neighbor obliges me:

1st **to forgive him all the evil he may have done me;**
2nd **neither to wish him nor to do him any evil;**
3rd **to procure for him all he needs for his soul and for his body.**

> NOTE: Jesus said: "As long as you did it to one of these My least brethren, you did it to Me." (Matthew 25:40)

FOR MY LIFE – I will do to others all the good that I would want them to do to me.

PRAYER – Act of Charity: "My God, grant me to love my neighbor as myself for love of Thee."

THE WORD OF GOD – "By this shall all men know that you are My disciples, if you have love one for another." (John 13:35)

Whoever gives simply a glass of water will not lose his reward

LITURGY – Notice that the celebrant and his assistants at High Mass give one another the kiss of peace after the Agnus Dei. This kiss is the sign of the charity which ought to unite all Christians as brothers.

ASSIGNMENT – Can one love his enemies from the heart? – How can one see that a Christian loves his enemies? – When did Jesus give the example of love for His enemies? – In what other ways can we show our charity toward our neighbor?

PROJECT – Make a series of friezes representing the acts of charity which you have done or witnessed.

Lesson 52

The First Commandment of God

"I am the Lord thy God, thou shalt not have strange gods before Me."

I. The Worship Due to God and to Jesus Christ

God is our Creator, our Master, and our Father. We should show Him our respect and our love by our thoughts, our words and our actions. We should adore Him.

Jesus is God and He has the right to our adoration. He was adored from His very birth.

The Gospel tells us about the adoration of the Magi: the star which they had seen in the East went before them until it stopped above the place where the Child was. They entered into the house, found the Child with Mary, His mother, and falling down they adored Him; then opening their treasures, they offered Him presents of gold, frankincense and myrrh.

Our Lord had given sight to the man born blind, who went away filled with happiness. Now it happened that Jesus met him again after the Jews, who were angry at the miracle, had chased him from the synagogue. Jesus said to him: "Dost thou believe in the Son of God?" He answered: "Who is He, Lord, that I may believe in Him?" And Jesus said to him: "Thou has both seen Him; and it is He that talketh with thee." And he said: "I believe, Lord." And falling down, he adored Him.[64]

REVIEW – Why must we adore God? – Does Jesus have a right to our adoration? – What did the Magi do in the presence of Jesus? – Repeat the little conversation between Jesus and the man born blind. What did the man do?

LESSON

• 336. *Recite the first commandment of God.*

I am the Lord thy God, thou shalt not have strange gods before Me.

---

[64] John 9:35-38

The First Commandment of God

† 337. *What does it mean to adore God?*

To adore God means to render Him the homage which we owe to Him as the Creator and Sovereign Master of all things.

> NOTE: "To render to God the honor which is due to Him" can also be said: "render to Him the worship which is due to Him."

† 338. *Should you adore Our Lord Jesus Christ?*

Yes, I should adore Our Lord Jesus Christ because He is God.

> NOTE: We should adore the Sacred Heart of Jesus because it is the heart of the Son of God made man.

339. *What sort of worship should you render to God?*

I should render to God an interior worship, an exterior worship and a public worship.

> NOTE: Interior worship is what I render to God in my soul, by my sentiments of adoration, of faith, of love, and of hope.
>
> Exterior worship is what I render to God when my body unites to my soul to adore God, for example, by making a sign of the cross, a genuflection, or a vocal prayer.
>
> Public worship is what is rendered in the name of the Church. When I assist at Mass, I participate in public worship.

340. *What are the principal acts of public worship?*

The principal acts of public worship are: Holy Mass, the recitation of the breviary, processions, and other ceremonies performed in the name of the Church.

341. *What are the sins against the adoration due to God?*

The sins against the adoration due to God are: idolatry, sacrilege, superstition, indifference, spiritism, and impiety.

> NOTE: <u>Idolatry</u> One sins by idolatry in adoring creatures instead of the Creator. Long ago, the pagans adored the sun.
>
> <u>Sacrilege</u> One sins by sacrilege in profaning holy things: receiving Communion in a state of mortal sin, or committing outrages against persons consecrated to God, for example striking a priest.
>
> <u>Superstition</u> One sins by superstition in believing that certain people or certain things have an extraordinary power which God did not give to them, for example the power to heal sicknesses or to make known the future.
>
> <u>Indifference</u> One sins by indifference in neglecting habitually one's religious duties such as prayer, the reception of the sacraments, or assistance at Mass on Sunday.
>
> <u>Spiritism</u> One sins gravely by spiritism when striving to make spirits speak, or to make things move by powers which can only come from the devil.

342. *What is the name of the virtue by which we render to God all the duties which we owe to Him?*

The virtue by which we render to God all of the duties which we owe to Him is the virtue of religion.

THE FIRST COMMANDMENT OF GOD

NOTE: "The word "religion" means "tying."
The virtue of religion "ties" us to God by adoration, thanksgiving, repentance, and supplication.

> **FOR MY LIFE** – I will keep a respectful silence in church. I will make with faith the genuflection which is a sign of adoration.
>
> **PRAYER** – My God, I adore You and I love You.
>
> **THE WORD OF GOD** – "The Lord thy God shalt thou adore, and Him only shalt thou serve." (Matthew 4:10)

LITURGY – You are part of a parish. The principal Offices which take place there are Mass, Vespers and Benediction of the Blessed Sacrament.

When you assist at these Offices you take part in the public worship which Christians ought to render to God.

ASSIGNMENT – You have noticed that one of your friends does not behave in church. What would you say to him to make him change his attitude?

PROJECT – Draw the design of the Temple in Jerusalem. Make an album of postcards showing the beautiful churches of Christendom, or the beautiful churches (of America), or the beautiful churches which you have visited.

Lesson 53

The First Commandment of God (Continued)

II. The Devotion Due to the Blessed Virgin and to the Saints

When the holy old man Simeon had taken in his arms the baby Jesus whom Mary was presenting in the Temple, he blessed God for having seen the Savior; then turning toward the Blessed Virgin, he said to her: "Thy own soul a sword shall pierce," a sword of sorrow.[65] The Blessed Virgin knew she would have to suffer; in advance, she united her sufferings to those of her Divine Son, for our salvation.

You see her suffer the most at the foot of the cross. She was there with Saint John. Jesus, when He saw Mary and the disciple whom He loved, said to His

---

[65] Luke 2:35

THE FIRST COMMANDMENT OF GOD (CONTINUED)

mother: "Woman, behold thy son." Then He said to the disciple: "Behold thy mother."[66]

Understand well what Jesus had just done: He gave His mother to us, because Saint John represented all humanity.

We are therefore the children of the Blessed Virgin.

We know that she takes care of us. Jesus willed that His first miracle be worked at the request of His mother. It was at Cana, in Galilee: Jesus, His disciples and the Blessed Virgin had been invited to a wedding. The wine was about to run out. Mary said to her Son: "They have no wine." You know the rest of the story: Jesus said to the waiters: "Fill the waterpots with water." They had six big stone jars there for water. They filled them up to the brim. Then Jesus said to them: "Draw out now and carry to the chief steward of the feast." They carried him some. When the chief steward had tasted the water made wine, not knowing whence it was, he said to the bridegroom: "Every man at first setteth forth good wine... But thou has kept the good wine until now."[67]

REVIEW – Who foretold to Mary that she would have to suffer? – How did this prediction come true? – Who gave Mary to us as our mother? – In what circumstances? – Tell the story of Jesus' first miracle. – What conclusion can you draw from it?

---

[66] John 19:25-27
[67] John 2:1-11

LESSON _____

• 343. *Should you honor the Most Blessed Virgin Mary more than the Angels and the Saints?*

Yes, I should honor the Most Blessed Virgin Mary more than the Angels and the Saints because she is the Mother of God and my mother also.

> NOTE: Carefully reread the chapter: "The Mystery of the Incarnation."

† 344. *How should you honor the Most Blessed Virgin?*

I should honor the Most Blessed Virgin by loving her as my mother, by praying to her with confidence, and by imitating her virtues.

> NOTE: To honor the Most Blessed Virgin, you can recite the rosary and the Angelus, wear her scapular and her medals, and go on pilgrimage to her shrines.

† 345. *Should you honor the Saints?*

Yes, I should honor the Saints because they are the friends of God and my protectors with Him.

> NOTE: We possess the bodies of a number of Saints, both men and women, either entirely or in fragments; we call these bodies relics, a word which means "remains."

The First Commandment of God (continued)

We honor the remains of the Saints and not those of all Christians because the Church assures us that the Saints are in heaven.

346. *Should you honor images of Our Lord, of the Most Blessed Virgin and of the Saints?*

Yes, I should honor images of Our Lord, of the Most Blessed Virgin and of the Saints because their images represent them.

> **NOTE:** When we kneel down before a fragment of the true cross or before a crucifix, it is not the cross which we adore but Jesus Christ, Who died for us on the cross.

FOR MY LIFE – I will do what I can to find a place of honor in the house, not only for the crucifix but also for a picture or a statue of the Most Blessed Virgin. I will always carry my rosary with me.

PRAYER – "Remember, O most gracious Virgin Mary, that never was it known that anyone who fled to thy protection, implored thy help or sought thy intercession was left unaided. Inspired by this confidence I fly unto thee, O Virgin of virgins, my Mother. To thee to I come, before thee I stand, sinful and sorrowful. O Mother of the Word Incarnate, despise not my petitions but in thy mercy hear and answer me. Amen."

THE WORD OF GOD – "Thou art all fair, O my love, and there is not a spot in thee." (Song of Songs 4:7)

LITURGY – The principal practices of devotion toward the Blessed Virgin are to celebrate her feast days with piety, to pray the rosary, and to wear the scapular or the medal which replaces it.

During the month of May, parishes follow the devotions of the month of Mary, and during the month of October they follow the month of the Rosary.

The relics of different Saints are venerated in every parish.

ASSIGNMENT – What are the different feasts in honor of the Most Blessed Virgin? – Describe the altar of the Blessed Virgin in your parish church. – Have you ever attended processions in her honor? Tell about them. – What are the pilgrimages to the shrines of the Most Blessed Virgin in America and England? – Who is the patron Saint of your parish? What do you know about him or her?

PROJECT – Make a picture album with beautiful copies of paintings or statues representing the Most Blessed Virgin.

LESSON 54

THE SECOND COMMANDMENT OF GOD

"Thou shalt not take the name of the Lord thy God in vain."

THE REVERENCE DUE TO THE NAME OF GOD

What do you say when you pray? You say: "Our Father, Who art in heaven, hallowed be Thy name..." The name of God is the holiest of all names. We must not say it lightly. In the Sermon on the Mount, Jesus reminded us of this rule. You know that swearing or taking an oath means taking God as a witness to what you say. Jesus said: "You have heard that it was said to them of old, thou shalt not forswear thyself: but thou shalt perform thy oaths to the Lord. But

I say to you not to swear at all, neither by heaven, for it is the throne of God, nor by the earth, for it is His footstool....Neither shalt thou swear by thy head, because thou canst not make one hair white or black. But let your speech be yea, yea: no, no: and that which is over and above these, is of evil."[68]

Yet, as you will see in the lesson, there are grave circumstances in which we are allowed to take an oath.

When you read the Passion of Our Lord, you will learn about the sin of the soldiers and of the Jews who mocked and insulted the Savior. They put a red cloak on His shoulders, a crown of thorns on His head, a reed in His hand, and they came before Him in turn, blaspheming and saying: "Hail, King of the Jews."

Those who blaspheme God now are imitating those miserable soldiers.

REVIEW – What do you say in the "Our Father"? – What did Jesus say about taking oaths? – When are we allowed to take an oath? – What was the sin of the soldiers and of the Jews during the Passion of Our Lord?

LESSON

- 347. *Recite the second commandment of God.*

Thou shalt not take the name of the Lord thy God in vain.

---

[68] Matthew 5:33-37

The Second Commandment of God

- 348. *What does the second commandment of God forbid us to do?*

The second commandment of God forbids us to take oaths in vain, to blaspheme, or to fail to fulfill the vows we have taken.

- 349. *What does it mean to swear or to take an oath?*

To swear or to take an oath means to take God as witness to what one affirms or what one promises.

> NOTE: It is permitted to take an oath when one has a serious reason, for example before a court of law.

- 350. *What is it to take an oath unlawfully?*

To take an oath unlawfully is to take God as witness of things without importance, or of things one knows to be false.

> NOTE: To take God as witness of things one knows to be false or evil is to wish to make God an accomplice to a lie or an injustice. That sin is called perjury.
>
> It is a sin to promise by oath a thing that is bad and it would be another sin to keep that promise.

- 351. *What is it to blaspheme?*

To blaspheme is to say insulting words about God, religion, or the Saints.

- 352. *What does it mean to make a vow?*

To make a vow is to promise God to accomplish a good work with the intention of obliging oneself under pain of sin.

NOTE: It is permitted to make vows on the condition of having seriously reflected and sought the advice of one's confessor.

FOR MY LIFE – Blasphemy is foul and insulting. I will never allow myself to utter such things. When I hear anyone blaspheming, I will try to make reparation by saying within myself: "God be praised," or "Blessed be God."

PRAYER – "Hallowed be Thy name…"

THE WORD OF GOD – "Every idle word that men shall speak, they shall render an account for it in the day of judgment." (Matthew 12:36)

LITURGY – During certain ceremonies, you can watch and notice that priests and faithful genuflect at the name of Jesus or bow their head.

ASSIGNMENT – One of your classmates developed a habit of blaspheming and swearing oaths about anything and everything. What would you say to him to make him change, and how can you make reparation for his insults against God?

PROJECT – Draw a filmstrip showing the denial of Saint Peter.

Lesson 55

The Third Commandment of God

"Remember thou keep holy the Lord's day."

The Sanctification of Sunday

God is our Creator. He has rights over us. All that He commands us to do is just and also contributes to our good.

He asks us to consecrate to Him one day per week; it is just because He is our Master. Yet He also acts as a Father, for the rest from work which He commands for Sunday renews the strength of our body, and assistance at Mass fosters the life of our soul.

Long ago, the Jews rested and prayed on Saturday. Since the time of the Apostles, this day is Sunday. When Jesus was a child He used to go to the synagogue with Saint Joseph and the Blessed Virgin, on the appointed day. At certain times of the year they also went to the Temple of Jerusalem.

You know what happened when He was twelve years old: Jesus stayed in the Temple while His mother and Saint Joseph, thinking Jesus was traveling with them in the same caravan, were returning home. After a day's journey, they realized that Jesus was not there. They went back to Jerusalem and, after three days, they found Him in the Temple in the middle of the doctors of the Law, listening to them and asking them questions. All those who heard Him were stupefied at His intelligence and His answers. At the sight of Him, His parents were struck with astonishment and Mary said to Him: "Son, why hast Thou done so to us? Behold Thy father and I have sought Thee sorrowing." Then Jesus said to them: "How is it that you sought Me? Did you not know that I must be about My Father's business?" (Luke 2:42-51)

On Sunday, every Christian should repeat after Jesus: "Above all, I should attend to the things of God."

REVIEW – Why can one say that the sanctification of Sunday is just and contributes to our good? – How did Jesus observe the day of the Lord? – What happened to Him when He was twelve? – What did the Blessed Virgin say to Him? – What did He answer?

LESSON

- 353. *Recite the third commandment of God.*

Remember thou keep holy the Lord's day.

The Third Commandment of God

† 354. *What should you do to sanctify Sunday?*

To sanctify Sunday, I should:

  1st assist at Mass;
  2nd not perform any forbidden works.

Otherwise, I would commit a serious sin.

• 355. *How should you assist at Mass?*

I should assist at Mass by hearing it completely, with faith, attention and devotion.

356. *Why should you not work on Sunday?*

I should not work on Sunday because it is the day of prayer and rest.

• 357. *Can you still perform certain works on Sunday?*

Yes, I can still perform certain works on Sunday, when they are necessary or authorized by a lawful custom.

> NOTE: Railroad companies may send off the trains listed on the schedule; farmers may gather a harvest threatened by a storm; the mother of a family may do the work necessary for the household.

358. *Do they commit a sin who make others work on Sunday without a serious reason?*

Yes, those people who make others work on Sunday without a serious reason commit a sin because they prevent their neighbor from obeying God.

359. Are recreational activities permitted on Sunday?

Yes, recreational activities are permitted on Sunday; they are even encouraged, provided they be appropriate and not prevent one from assisting at Mass.

> **FOR MY LIFE** – I will never forget that Sunday is not a day which belongs to me, but the day which is set aside for the Lord. I will not be content merely with giving Him what He commands, by assisting at Mass. That day will be specially consecrated to the study of religion, to prayer, and to recreations that can raise up my soul.
>
> **PRAYER** – "Hallowed be Thy name..."
>
> **THE WORD OF GOD** – "Did you not know that I must be about My Father's business?" (Luke 2:49)

LITURGY – High Mass or Solemn Mass is different from Low Mass. Certain parts are chanted either by the priest (such as the Preface) or by the choir (such as the Introit) or by the faithful (such as the Credo).

The priest at Solemn Masses is assisted by a deacon and a subdeacon. There are incensings. The pastor also makes the announcements and gives a sermon.

ASSIGNMENT – Describe the Sunday of a good Christian.

PROJECT – Make two filmstrips: one showing Sunday, "Day of the Lord," the other showing Sunday, "Day of man."

Lesson 56

The Fourth Commandment of God

"Honor thy father and thy mother."

I. Duties of Children Toward Their Parents

After telling what happened to Jesus when He was twelve years old, the Gospel summarizes the life of Jesus in Nazareth in these few words: "And He went down with them and came to Nazareth and was subject to them.

"And His mother kept all these things in her heart. And Jesus advanced in wisdom and age and grace with God and men."[69]

In a letter to the Christians of Ephesus, Saint Paul recalls the duties of children and of parents, and he writes: "Children, obey your parents in the Lord: for this is just.

"Honor thy father and thy mother, which is the first commandment with a promise: 'That it may be well with thee, and thou mayest be long lived upon earth.'

"And you, fathers, provoke not your children to anger: but bring them up in the discipline and correction of the Lord."[70]

How can you imitate Jesus? The lesson which you are about to study will show you. Four words sum up your duties: love, respect, obedience, assistance.

REVIEW – What do you know about the life of Jesus in Nazareth? – What do you notice in the statements of Saint Paul to the Ephesians? – What words sum up your duties toward your parents?

LESSON

- **360. Recite the fourth commandment of God. Honor thy father and thy mother.**

---

[69] Luke 2:51-52
[70] Ephesians 6:1-4

The Fourth Commandment of God

361. Why should you honor your father and your mother?

I should honor my father and my mother because they gave me life and because they take the place of God for me.

† 362. What should you do to honor your father and your mother?

To honor my father and my mother, I should love them, respect them, obey them, and help them.

• *363. What should you do in order to love your parents genuinely?*

In order to love my parents genuinely, I should wish for them and do for them the most good possible.

• *364. What should you do in order to respect your parents?*

In order to respect my parents, I should be polite to them and endure with patience their weaknesses and even their faults.

• *365. What should you do in order to obey your parents well?*

In order to obey my parents well, I should do all that they command, quickly, precisely, and without complaining.

• *366. How would you fail in your duty to help your parents?*

I would fail in my duty to help my parents:

1st by refusing to assist them.
2nd by abandoning them if they were poor, sick or infirm.
3rd by neglecting to obtain religious help for them in case of need.

• 367. *Do you have duties toward the other members of your family?*

Yes, I have duties toward the other members of my family: I should above all respect my grandparents, love my brothers and sisters and give them a good example.

• 368. *Do you owe respect and obedience to other people besides your parents?*

Yes, I owe respect and obedience to my spiritual and temporal superiors.

> NOTE: We owe respect and obedience to our spiritual and temporal superiors because they represent God.
>
> A child should respect his teachers, speak of them without meanness and obey them in everything which they have the right to command.

II. Duties of Parents Toward Their Children

369. *What should parents do for the soul of their children?*

Parents should have their children baptized as soon as possible, raise them in a Christian man-

The Fourth Commandment of God

ner, correct their faults, and give them a good example.

>NOTE: In order to raise their children in a Christian manner, parents should:
>
>1st instruct them in the truths of the faith and ensure that they attend catechism classes;
>
>2nd Confide their education to Christian teachers, if it is possible.

370. *What should parents do for the body of their children?*

Parents should watch over the life and health of their children.

FOR MY LIFE – I will consider the pain which I have caused to my parents and I will seek to cause them as much joy as possible, by my behavior and my work.

PRAYER – My God, grant that I may never live selfishly and that I may think of the happiness of my parents before thinking of my own.

THE WORD OF GOD – "And (Jesus) went down with (His parents) and came to Nazareth and was subject to them." (Luke 2:51)

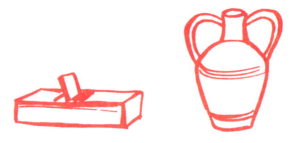

With Jesus, serve others

LITURGY – Christian families have Masses celebrated for their deceased relatives, (especially on the anniversary of their death.)

ASSIGNMENT – Why should you love your parents? – Why should you respect your parents? – Why should you obey your parents? – Why should you help your parents? – How can you help your parents, beginning even now? – What can you do for them later?

PROJECT – Construct a diorama representing the workshop of Nazareth. Make a set of cards or a puzzle showing the occupations of the Child Jesus, model of docility.

Lesson 57

The Fourth Commandment of God (Continued)

III. Duties Toward One's Homeland and Toward All Men

There is a page in the Gospel which shows us all the love of Jesus for His homeland. He drew near to Jerusalem, the great city with its white houses and with its Temple etched out on the horizon. He gazed upon the city and wept over it, saying: "Jerusalem, Jerusalem, thou that killest the prophets and stonest them that are sent unto thee, how often would I have gathered together thy children, as the hen doth gather her chickens under her wings, and thou wouldst not?…If thou also hadst known, and that in this thy day, the things that are to thy peace: but now they are hidden from thy eyes. For the days shall come upon thee: and thy enemies shall cast a trench about thee and compass thee round and straiten thee on every side, and beat thee flat to the ground, and thy children who are in thee. And they shall not leave in thee a stone upon a stone: because thou hast not known the time of thy visitation." (Matthew 23:37, Luke 19:41-44)

Jesus loved His homeland and He wept when He thought of the ruin of Jerusalem. You, too, have a homeland; it is like an extended family for you. It gives you its soil, its treasures of art; it protects you by its laws, police, and army. Love it. Your duty right now is to work in order to become an excellent citizen; and to do so, be first of all a perfect Christian.

However, yours is not the only nation in the world. All around her, others live and develop. All nations together form the immense family which is called Humanity. It was redeemed by the Blood of Jesus Christ, Who said to His Apostles: "Go, teach all nations." You should love all men as brothers; it is the commandment of Jesus: "Love one another."

REVIEW – What was the homeland of Jesus? – How do you see that He loved it? – What is your present duty toward your homeland? – Toward humanity?

LESSON

- 371. *What are a person's duties toward his homeland?*

A person's duties toward his homeland are to respect the civil authority, obey just laws and conscientiously fulfill all civic duties.

> NOTE: The principal civic duties are to pay taxes, to defend one's country even at the price of one's blood, and to fulfill one's electoral duty according to one's conscience.

THE FOURTH COMMANDMENT OF GOD (CONTINUED)

- 372. *To what does the electoral duty oblige?*

The electoral duty obliges one to vote for capable men and, if possible, for Christians.

> NOTE: It can be a sin not to vote, for he who does not vote may be a cause of bad candidates' coming into power.

- 373. *Do you have duties toward the men of foreign countries?*

Yes, I have duties toward the men of foreign countries because they are my brothers and because Jesus Christ said: "Love one another."

- 374. *What are your duties toward all men of foreign countries?*

My duties toward all men of foreign countries are to respect their rights and work to maintain peace.

> NOTE: War is indeed a very great misfortune, because it too easily leads to injustice, hatred, violence, and sorrow for everyone. In case of war you should do all of your duty and sacrifice your personal interest to the interest of all, even to giving your life for your country.

- 375. *Does the State have duties toward its citizens?*

Yes, the State has duties toward its citizens: it must maintain order and public services, and by its laws, protect workers against unemployment, sickness, and accidents, and assist the elderly.

> **FOR MY LIFE** – Our Lord died for all men yet He loved His homeland. Faithful to the law of charity toward all, I will love my country with predilection and I will give her all that she may ask of me when the time comes, including even my life.
>
> **PRAYER** – My God, give peace and order to my country and to all nations.
>
> **THE WORD OF GOD** – "Render therefore to Caesar the things that are Caesar's, and to God, the things that are God's." (Matthew 22:21)

LITURGY – Every year on the Feast of Christ the King, the Church has us recite the act of consecration of the human race to the Sacred Heart of Jesus. Christians therefore pray for the great human family.

ASSIGNMENT – Who is the Patron Saint of your country? – Who is the Patron Saint of your diocese? – Who are the secondary Patrons of your country? – On what days does one celebrate the feast of these saints? – Who are the other saints particularly honored in your country? – Who are the Patron Saints of your parish? – How should one honor them?

Lesson 58

The Fifth Commandment of God

"Thou shalt not kill."

Respect for Life

When you hear the story of a crime, you think to yourself: "How can a man have done that?" Reflect: Why did Cain kill his brother Abel? Because he was jealous of him.

How can a man commit a crime? Long ago, that same man was a child like you. He did not think about committing crime, but he let feelings of envy and jealousy grow in his heart; he did not want to forgive, he was cruel, he only thought about himself. He let his passions grow in himself; he only wanted to enjoy without wanting to mortify himself. One day, in order to get revenge, in order to satisfy his passions, he killed someone. If he had fought against his evil tendencies, he would have stayed an honest man.

Our life belongs to God. Under no circumstances are we allowed to kill ourselves. Judas betrayed his Master; he suddenly understood the horror of his action, he felt disgust at the thought of it, he knew that everyone would despise him; he did not think of asking forgiveness, but tied a rope to the branch of a tree and hanged himself. Did he have the right to kill himself? No, he did not have that right. His life still belonged to God, and he could have turned toward repentance; by killing himself, he cast himself into hell.

God is present in a soul in the state of grace; this divine presence is the life of the soul. Mortal sin destroys this life. We should therefore take care to keep it far from our soul and from the souls of others, for we can kill the soul of our neighbor by inciting him to sin by our words, our gestures, our writings, or our examples. To do so is a grave sin which is called scandal.

"Woe to that man by whom the scandal cometh," said Jesus. "It were better for him that a millstone should be hanged about his neck, and that he should be drowned in the depth of the sea."[71]

REVIEW – Why did Cain kill his brother? – How can a man come to commit a crime? – Why did Judas not have the right to hang himself? – Who dwells in a soul in the state of grace? – What did Our Lord say about those who lead others into sin?

---

[71] Matthew 18:6-7

THE FIFTH COMMANDMENT OF GOD

LESSON

- 376. *Recite the fifth commandment of God.*

Thou shalt not kill.

- 377. *What does the fifth commandment of God forbid you to do?*

The fifth commandment of God forbids me to do anything that may harm the life of the body or of the soul, in myself or in my neighbor.

378. *How could you harm your neighbor in his body?*

I could harm my neighbor in his body by killing him willfully or by imprudence, by wounding him or by striking him unjustly.

> NOTE: Killing is sometimes permitted:
>
> 1st to punish a criminal condemned in a court of law;
>
> 2nd to defend one's homeland against the enemy;
>
> 3rd to defend oneself against an evil-doer, when one cannot save one's life by any other means.

379. *How could you harm your neighbor in his soul?*

I could harm my neighbor in his soul by scandal, that is to say, by drawing him into sin by my words, my writing or my example.

• **380.** *Is it a great sin gravely to scandalize one's neighbor?*

Yes, it is a great sin gravely to scandalize one's neighbor, for it means exposing him to committing a mortal sin, that is to say to losing supernatural life.

381. *Would you be responsible for the sins which you caused to be committed by gravely scandalizing your neighbor?*

Yes, I would be responsible for the sins which I caused to be committed by gravely scandalizing my neighbor, and God would hold me accountable.

> NOTE: Jesus said: "Woe to that man by whom the scandal cometh. It were better for him that a millstone should be hanged about his neck, and that he should be drowned in the depth of the sea." (Matthew 18:6-7)

382. *What is suicide?*

Suicide is the crime of those who willfully kill themselves.

> NOTE: 1st Suicide is a great sin, for God alone is the Master of our life. It is a form of cowardice in the face of a painful duty.
>
> 2nd Those who fight in a duel are guilty, for they put themselves in danger of being killed and they seek to kill or wound their adversary.

THE FIFTH COMMANDMENT OF GOD

383. *Are you allowed to make animals suffer for no reason?*

No, I am not allowed to make animals suffer for no reason. Making them suffer uselessly is an act of cruelty.

> FOR MY LIFE – I will never keep a desire for revenge in my heart, remembering that Jesus gave to all of His disciples the commandment to love even their enemies.
>
> PRAYER – "O Lord, shower Thy blessings on my friends and on my enemies."
>
> THE WORD OF GOD – "Woe to that man by whom the scandal cometh." (Matthew 18:7)

LITURGY – The Church instituted special prayers, called the "Forty Hours' Devotion," to make reparation for the scandals of the Carnival (public festivals before Ash Wednesday). These prayers, recited before the Blessed Sacrament solemnly exposed, tell us very clearly that the Church shares in Jesus' horror of scandal.

ASSIGNMENT – May one defend one's life by killing another? – What are the goods more precious than life and for which God permits us to sacrifice our own life? – People sometimes say that a person "had the courage" to do away with his own life. Is suicide an act of courage or of cowardice?

PROJECT – Construct a diorama about Cain and Abel.

LESSON 59

THE SIXTH AND NINTH COMMANDMENTS OF GOD

"Thou shalt not commit adultery."
"Thou shalt not covet thy neighbor's wife."

PURITY

There is a phrase Jesus once said, which you should know by heart: "Blessed are the pure of heart, for they shall see God."

Jesus showed us those who are pure of heart: they are the little children, and He gave them to us as models. One day, some mothers were bringing their young children to Him that He might embrace them and lay His hands upon them to bless them, but the disciples tried to turn them away. Jesus was greatly displeased and said to them: "Suffer the little children to come unto Me and forbid them not: for the kingdom of heaven is for such."[72]

Why do these little children have the kingdom of God in them? It is because they do not have bad thoughts, or look at bad things; they commit no wicked gestures or wicked actions; they say no words against purity.

One cannot always remain a child but one can always remain pure, and Jesus gives us the means to do so: "Watch and pray," He said. Watch over your eyes, for there are things you should not see; watch over your ears, for there are words you should not hear; watch over your tongue, for there are conversations which you should not have. Watch over your hands – no familiarity or forbidden games. When you are bigger, there will be many occasions of danger and you must avoid them courageously; that is what Jesus meant by these words: "If thy eye scandalize thee, pluck it out, and cast it from thee. It is better for thee having one eye to enter into life, than having two eyes to be cast into hell fire." (Matthew 18:9)

Pray to Jesus, pray to the Blessed Virgin Mary.

REVIEW – What will those who are pure of heart see? – Why did Jesus give us little children as our models? – Why must we watch and pray in order to remain pure? – What did Jesus say about occasions of danger?

---

[72] Mark 10:13-14; Matthew 19:13-14

THE SIXTH AND NINTH COMMANDMENTS OF GOD

LESSON _____

• 384. *Recite the sixth and ninth commandments.*

Thou shalt not commit adultery. Thou shalt not covet thy neighbor's wife.

• 385. *What does the virtue of purity forbid you to do?*

The virtue of purity forbids me any thoughts, desires, looks, words, reading, or actions which may stain my soul and my body.

> NOTE: Impure thoughts and desires are not sins when we do not seek them and when we do not willfully keep them in our mind. In case of doubt, we need to ask our confessor.

• 386. *Would you sin by accepting occasions of impurity?*

Yes, I would sin by accepting occasions of impurity, in particular by watching bad shows or movies on television, by reading bad magazines, or by spending time with friends who would lead me to do so.

> NOTE: Idleness and intemperance as well as immodest dress, attitudes or dances are also occasions of impurity.

387. *Why is impurity a sin?*

Impurity is a sin because it stains both body and soul, which had become by grace the dwelling-place of the Holy Ghost.

• 388. *What are the principal means to avoid impurity?*

The principal means to avoid impurity are mortification, prayer, Confession, frequent Communion, devotion to the Blessed Virgin, and the fleeing of dangerous occasions.

> FOR MY LIFE – I will take special care to avoid bad books, bad movies and bad companions, and I will have a great devotion to the Blessed Virgin.
>
> PRAYER – "Grant me, my God, never to forget that my body has become a 'temple of the Holy Ghost' and that I am a 'member of Christ.' Mother most pure, pray for us."
>
> THE WORD OF GOD – "Blessed are the clean of heart: for they shall see God." (Matthew 5:8)

**This demon
– impurity –
can only be cast out
by prayer and fasting**

The Sixth and Ninth Commandments of God

LITURGY – In all of Her liturgical prayers, the Church places great value on the virtue of purity. She sings the praises of Mary, the Virgin most pure. She has a special office for virgins.

The virgin martyrs most honored in the Church are Saint Agnes, Saint Agatha, Saint Lucy, Saint Cecilia and Saint Catherine.

ASSIGNMENT – Is there one Apostle whom Jesus loved more than the others? Why? – What did Jesus promise to those who kept their hearts pure? – What is the greatest threat to your purity? – Who can help you the most to remain pure?

PROJECT – Make a leaflet representing the scenes of the life of Saint John the Evangelist. Make a set of friezes representing Jesus and little children.

Lesson 60

The Seventh and Tenth Commandments of God

"Thou shalt not steal."
"Thou shalt not covet thy neighbor's goods."

The Material Goods of Our Neighbor

One day a man named Zaccheus, the leader of the publicans and extremely rich, received Our Lord in his home. He stood up before Jesus and said to Him: "Behold, Lord, the half of my goods I give to the poor; and if I have wronged any man of any thing, I restore him fourfold."[73] Jesus was happy to hear these words. Indeed, they tell us that Zaccheus considered all the goods of the earth as belonging first to God, Who confides them to certain people for their personal use and for the good of oth-

---

[73] Luke 19:8

ers. Zaccheus certainly thought so because he gave half of his fortune to the poor. They also show that this man considered it a sin to wrong someone in his material goods, since he punished himself by giving back four times as much.

Zaccheus was a truly honest man. He gave to each one what was his due. You want to become an honest adult some day. Start learning about justice already, at school, at home, in your daily life. Watch over yourself and be sure you respect the rights of others in the smallest details, and later on you will be able to walk with your head held high and your conscience free from all reproach.

REVIEW – What did Zaccheus say to Jesus? – Why was Jesus happy to hear these words? – What did Zaccheus do when he had wronged someone? – What resolutions can you take in order to remain always honest?

LESSON

- 389. *Recite the seventh and the tenth commandments of God.*

Thou shalt not steal. Thou shalt not covet thy neighbor's goods.

- 390. *What do the seventh and the tenth commandments of God forbid you to do?*

The seventh and the tenth commandments of God forbid me to take, to keep, to damage, or even to desire unjustly what belongs to my neighbor.

391. *At whose service ought the goods of the earth to be?*

The goods of the earth ought to be at the service of all men.

392. *To whom do the goods of the earth belong?*

The goods of the earth belong to God Who created them and to those who lawfully possess them.

> NOTE: 1st Those who lawfully possess the goods of the earth are those who have acquired them by their work or by inheritance or by some other honest means.
>
> 2nd Since the goods of the earth ought to be at the service of all men, those who possess them do not have the right to use them for themselves alone in a selfish manner; they ought to make others benefit from them.
>
> 3rd The Popes have often expressed the desire that all men of the earth might own property.

• 393. *What are those who unjustly take the goods of their neighbor?*

Those who unjustly take the goods of their neighbor are thieves, and so are all those who deprive someone of what is due to him.

> NOTE: The following men deprive someone of what is due to him:
>
> 1st merchants who deceive as to the weight or the quality of their merchandise;
>
> 2nd those who carry out unjust lawsuits;
>
> 3rd employers who do not pay a just wage;
>
> 4th workers who do not work as they should.

The Seventh and Tenth Commandments of God

● 394. *Who are those who unjustly keep the goods of their neighbor?*

Those who unjustly keep the goods of their neighbor are those who do not pay their debts, who do not give back what they have taken, or who simply keep what they have found.

● 395. *What are they who have unjustly taken or kept the goods of their neighbor obliged to do?*

They who have unjustly taken or kept the goods of their neighbor are obliged to return the stolen property as soon as possible.

> NOTE: They also wrong their neighbor in his goods who unjustly damage or destroy what belongs to him. They, too, are obliged to repair the damage caused.

FOR MY LIFE – I will never take the least little thing which does not belong to me, even from my parents, remembering that it would mean I was learning the habit of indelicacy and thievery. I will have a horror of copying the work of others at school, for it is also an indelicacy and an injustice. For the same reason, I will never cheat at games.

PRAYER – "O my God, You Who see all things even to our most secret thoughts, grant that neither my hands nor my heart ever commit injustice."

THE WORD OF GOD – "He that is faithful in that which is least is faithful also in that which is greater; and he that is unjust in that which is little is unjust also in that which is greater." (Luke 16:10)

LITURGY – The Church has always encouraged spending money for the embellishment of churches, sacred vessels, and vestments intended for use at the Holy Sacrifice, for the goods of the earth belong first to God. It is a way of thanking Him for what He gives us every day in great abundance.

ASSIGNMENT – You have seen one of your friends copying during a test. What would you say to her to keep her from doing it ever again?

PROJECT – Make a series of drawings on the parable of the workers in the vineyard.

LESSON 61

THE EIGHTH COMMANDMENT OF GOD

"Thou shalt not bear false witness against thy neighbor."

HONESTY AND OUR NEIGHBOR'S REPUTATION

The Apostle Saint James wrote the following statement in a letter to the first Christians: "If any man offend not in word, the same is a perfect man. He is able also with a bridle to lead about the whole body." He compares the tongue to the helm of a ship. He also says: "By the tongue we bless God and the Father; and by it we curse men who are made after the likeness of God."[74]

---

[74] James 3:2-4, 9

It must not be so with us. Throughout this chapter, you are going to see the different sins of the tongue: lying, as Herod did, who learned of the birth of Jesus from the Magi and thought to himself: "I want to kill that child," while he said to the Magi: "Come and tell me where He is, that I, too, might adore Him"; bearing false witness, as did the Jews before the judgment seat of Pilate: "This man Jesus is stirring up the people against the authority, pushing them to revolt, forbidding them to pay tribute to Caesar."

Calumny and detraction are other sins of the tongue. Jesus forbids us to commit these sins; He forbids us even to judge others: "Judge not, that you may not be judged. For with what judgment you judge, you shall be judged," and He points out that we are poor judges: "Why seest thou the mote that is in thy brother's eye, and seest not the beam that is in thy own eye? Or how sayest thou to thy brother: 'Let me cast the mote out of thy eye'; and behold a beam is in thy own eye? Thou hypocrite, cast out first the beam out of thy own eye, and then shalt thou see to cast out the mote out of thy brother's eye." (Matthew 7:1-5)

REVIEW – Which Apostle wrote about sins of the tongue? – To what does he compare the tongue? – What lie did Herod tell? – What sin did the Jews commit before the judgment seat of Pilate? – What did Jesus say about judgments we make against others?

THE EIGHTH COMMANDMENT OF GOD

LESSON

- 396. *Recite the eighth commandment of God.*

Thou shalt not bear false witness against thy neighbor.

- 397. *What does the eighth commandment of God forbid you to do?*

The eighth commandment of God forbids me:
  1st to lie;
  2nd to bear false witness before a court of law;
  3rd to damage the reputation of my neighbor.

† 398. *What does it mean to lie?*

To lie is to speak the contrary of what one is thinking, with the intention to deceive.

† 399. *Is lying permitted?*

No, lying is never permitted, not even to excuse oneself or to help someone.

> NOTE: It is not lying to refuse to reveal the truth under certain circumstances:
>
> 1st in order to keep a secret which one must not reveal. For example a doctor or a notary must keep the secrets of their clients; a confessor must keep the secret of the confessional;
>
> 2nd in order to defend one's country against an unjust enemy;
>
> 3rd in order to defend oneself against an evildoer when one cannot safeguard one's life or goods in any other way.

- 400. *What does it mean to bear false witness before a court of law?*

To bear false witness before a court of law means to lie when one is called upon to be a witness.

401. *How can you damage your neighbor in his reputation?*

I can damage my neighbor in his reputation by calumny, detraction or rash judgment.

- 402. *What is calumny?*

Calumny is accusing one's neighbor of a fault which he does not possess or a sin which he did not commit.

- 403. *What is detraction?*

Detraction is making known without necessity the sins or defects of one's neighbor.

- 404. *What is rash judgment of one's neighbor?*

Rash judgment of one's neighbor is thinking ill of others without sufficient proof.

405. *Must we keep certain secrets?*

Yes, we must keep secrets, under pain of sin.

> NOTE: Someone who has wronged his neighbor by false witness, calumny, detraction, or violation of a secret is obliged in conscience to repair the damage done to his neighbor, as far as possible.

The Eighth Commandment of God

> **For my life** – I will have the greatest esteem for honesty and I will never lie, even to excuse myself.
>
> **Prayer** – My God, give me the courage to tell the truth, even when it is not in my favor.
>
> **The Word of God** – "But let your speech be yea, yea: no, no: and that which is over and above these, is of evil." (Matthew 5:37)

Liturgy – As the priest is incensing the altar, he says to God: "Set a watch, O Lord, before my mouth, and a door round about my lips, that my heart not incline to evil words."

Assignment – One who lies sins against which virtues? – One who bears false witness sins against which virtues? – One who detracts sins against which virtues? – One who calumniates sins against which virtues? – One who makes a rash judgment sins against which virtues?

Project – Construct a stage with movable characters representing the parable of the mote and the beam.

LESSON 62

THE PRECEPTS OF THE CHURCH

Have you ever watched a shepherd guarding his sheep? He leads them into a field and obliges them to stay there. When the grass becomes more sparse, he moves them to a different place; in the evening, he herds them into shelters under the guard of watchful dogs. Now remember what Jesus said to Saint Peter: "Feed My lambs, feed My sheep," and you will understand that the Pope, head of the Church, ought to fulfill the functions of a true shepherd by making laws.

The Church has been faithful to this mission, since the Apostles from the very beginning made precepts forbidding the faithful to observe the Jewish laws any longer; when they replaced Saturday, the day of rest dedicated to the Lord, by Sunday, which recalled the resurrection of Christ; when they indicated the proper way of doing penance.

These laws of the Church have allowed Christians better to observe the commandments of God.

The Precepts of the Church

As you study the six precepts which are the object of today's lesson, you will notice that the Church acts as a good mother who helps us better to adore our Creator, to keep our soul pure, to draw us nearer to Jesus in the Eucharist, and to perform penance pleasing to God.

Be obedient children and remember all your life the words of Our Lord to His Apostles: "He that heareth you heareth Me; and he that despiseth you despiseth Me."[75]

REVIEW – What does a shepherd do for the good of his sheep? – What did Jesus say to Saint Peter? – Did the Church make laws from the very beginning? – Why should you obey the Church?

LESSON

• 406. *Does the Church have the right to give precepts?*

Yes, the Church has the right to give precepts, and Jesus Christ said that to disobey the Church is to disobey Himself.

> NOTE: The Church gives us precepts in order to help us better to obey the Gospel and the commandments of God.

† 407. *Recite the precepts of the Church.*

1st   To assist at Mass on all Sundays and holy days of obligation;

---

[75] Luke 10:16

2nd To fast and to abstain on the days appointed (by the Church);
3rd To confess our sins at least once a year;
4th To receive Holy Communion during the Easter time;
5th To contribute to the support of the Church;
6th To observe the laws of the Church concerning marriage.

• 408. *What does the first precept of the Church command you to do?*

The first precept of the Church commands me to dedicate to God the feasts of obligation as one dedicates Sunday to Him.

• 409. *What are the six holy days of obligation for the United States of America?*

The six holy days of obligation for the United States of America are:
  – **the Feast of the Immaculate Conception of the Blessed Virgin Mary, December 8th;**
  – **Christmas, December 25th, the feast of the birth of the Savior;**
  – **the Octave Day of the Nativity, January 1st, the Feast of the Circumcision;**
  – **Ascension Day, 40 days after Easter, the day on which Christ ascended into heaven;**
  – **the Feast of the Assumption, August 15th, when we celebrate the Blessed Virgin Mary raised up into heaven, body and soul;**
  – **the Feast of All Saints, November 1st.**

THE PRECEPTS OF THE CHURCH

● 410. *What else does the first precept of the Church command you to do?*

The first precept of the Church also commands me to assist at Mass on Sundays and holy days of obligation, under pain of mortal sin.

> NOTE: Assistance at Vespers and other ceremonies is recommended by the Church.

† 411. *When does the Church command you to go to Confession?*

The Church commands me to go to Confession at least once a year, after the age of reason.

† 412. *When does the Church command you to receive Communion?*

The Church commands me to receive Communion once every year, at Easter time, after the age of reason.

● 413. *Is it a grave sin not to perform one's Easter duty?*

Yes, it is a grave sin not to perform one's Easter duty, for it would be disobeying Jesus Christ and the Church.

> NOTE: We must remember the words of Jesus: "Except you eat the Flesh of the Son of Man and drink His Blood, you shall not have life in you."[76]

414. *On what days does the Church command a fast?*

The Church commands a fast during Lent, on Ash Wednesday and on Good Friday.

---

[76] John 6:54

NOTE: One is bound to fast from the age of 18 to the age of 60. One is dispensed from fasting if one is in ill health or must perform difficult labor.

415. *What does it mean to fast?*

To fast is to have only one main meal a day, to which one may add, in the morning and evening, what is absolutely necessary to perform one's duty of state.

> NOTE: 1st One must fast from the age of eighteen to the age of sixty.
>
> 2nd One is dispensed from fasting when one is in ill health or must perform difficult labor.
>
> 3rd Lent was instituted in memory of the fast of Our Lord in the desert; it lasts forty days, from Ash Wednesday to Holy Saturday (at noon).
>
> 4th There also exist three days of penance called Ember Days: Wednesday, Friday and Saturday, placed at the beginning of the each season of the year.

416. *On what days does the Church command abstinence?*

The Church forbids us to eat meat on Friday of each week, on Ash Wednesday, (Vigils of some feasts, and Ember Days).

> NOTE: 1st We should abstain from the age of fourteen years.
>
> 2nd If a holy day of obligation, namely the Immaculate Conception, Christmas, the Octave of the Nativity, the Ascension, or the Assumption, falls on a Friday, one may eat meat on that day.

The Precepts of the Church

3rd The Church commands us to fast or to refrain from eating meat in a spirit of penance.

> **FOR MY LIFE** – To assist at Mass on Sunday and holy days of obligation, go to Confession every year, receive Communion at Easter, and fast and abstain on the appointed days, are a minimum which every Christian must observe if he wishes to obey the Church. I want to be a good Christian, so that is why I promise this obedience throughout my life.
>
> **PRAYER** – Grant me, O God, the courage to obey the Church in spite of human respect, which is only a form of cowardice.
>
> **THE WORD OF GOD** – "If he will not hear the Church, let him be to thee as the heathen." (Matthew 18:17)

LITURGY – Remember that the Church established the Ember Day fasts at the beginning of each season of the year in order to draw down the blessings of God on the ordination of priests and the labors of the faithful.

ASSIGNMENT – Name the feast which recalls the day:
- on which the Blessed Virgin Mary was conceived without sin;
- on which Jesus was born;
- on which Jesus ascended into heaven;
- on which the Blessed Virgin was lifted up into heaven.

When:
1. should you abstain?
2. should you fast?
3. should you do penance?
4. should you go to Confession?

PROJECT – Design a stained-glass window illustrating the precepts of the Church.

Lesson 63

Sin

Do you want to understand what sin is? Follow Jesus step by step from the manger to the cross. He came to earth to do the will of His Father and to take away the sins of the world. Sin was such a great evil that suffering became inseparable from Christ.

He suffered from poverty and cold in the cave where He was born. He suffered on account of His hard work as a carpenter in the workshop of Nazareth. He suffered in His last three years on earth from the troubles and persecutions of which He was the victim. He suffered a terrible agony in the Garden of Olives.

On that evening of Holy Thursday, He was a stone's throw away from His sleeping Apostles. He could see all the sins of the world in His divine gaze – the sins of the past, those of the present, those of the future and He could but say: "My soul is sorrowful, even unto death." Three times He said to His Father: "My

Father, if it be possible, let this chalice pass from Me. Yet not My will, but Thine be done."

So great was His suffering that His sweat became as drops of blood, trickling down upon the ground. Then Judas came to betray Him with a kiss, and here you can see all the ingratitude of sin. Then came the arrest, the judgment, the scourging, the crowning with thorns, the way of Calvary, the crucifixion, the last sufferings, and death.

It was for our sins that Christ humbled Himself, that He obeyed the will of His Father even unto death, and the death of the cross.

REVIEW – How did Jesus suffer when He was a tiny baby? – When He was living in Nazareth? – When He was preaching? – During His last days? – Why did He suffer so much?

LESSON

† 417. *What do you do when you disobey a commandment of God or of the Church, knowing you are doing it and wanting to do it?*

When I disobey a commandment of God or of the Church, knowing it and willing it, I commit a sin.

• 418. *Is temptation a sin?*

No, temptation is not a sin if one does not consent to it.

SIN

419. *In how many ways can one commit a sin?*

One can commit a sin by thought, word, action, and omission.

† 420. *How many kinds of sin are there?*

There are two kinds of sin: mortal sin and venial sin.

† 421. *When would you commit a mortal sin?*

I would commit a mortal sin if:
- I disobeyed God in a grave matter;
- I knew it was grave (knowledge);
- I accepted to sin anyway (consent).

• 422. *Why is that kind of sin called mortal?*

That kind of sin is called mortal because it takes supernatural life away from the soul, making us enemies of God and worthy of hell.

• 423. *What should you do if you have had the misfortune of committing a mortal sin?*

If I have had the misfortune of committing a mortal sin, I should make an act of perfect contrition, go to Confession as soon as possible, and take the means not to commit it again.

† 424. *When would you commit a venial sin?*

I would commit a venial sin if I disobeyed God in a slight matter; or even in a grave matter, if I did not fully know it was grave, or if I did not fully know what I was doing.

- 425. *Why is that kind of sin called venial?*

That kind of sin is called venial because it does not take away supernatural life; but it inclines us toward mortal sin and makes us deserve temporal punishment, which we will have to suffer in this world or the next.

426. *What do you call an "occasion of sin"?*

I call an "occasion of sin" anything that can lead me into sin.

> NOTE: Occasions of sin are bad examples, bad companions, bad books or magazines, bad conversations, bad shows or movies.

> FOR MY LIFE – By mortal sin, I oppose my will to that of God; by venial sin I oppose my good pleasure to the desire of God. When I am tempted to oppose myself to God in this way, I will think of all that sin cost Jesus Christ, "obedient even unto death, and to the death of the cross."
>
> PRAYER – "Holy Ghost, eternal source of light, dispel the darkness which hides from me the ugliness and the wickedness of sin. Grant me, my God, to conceive so great a horror for sin that I might hate it, if it were possible, as much as You hate it Yourself and that I might fear nothing so much as committing it in the future."
>
> THE WORD OF GOD – "Watch ye: and pray that ye enter not into temptation. The spirit indeed is willing, but the flesh is weak." (Matthew 26:41)

Sin

Liturgy – Several times during the Mass (at the two "Confiteors," at the "Lavabo," at the "Domine non sum dignus"), the Church has us ask forgiveness for our sins. Do we think about what we are saying?

Assignment – What does mortal sin make us lose? – Can one lose anything of greater value? – Is it an exaggeration to say that there is no greater misfortune? Why? – Does venial sin have the same consequence? – What harm does it do to our soul?

Project – Design a frieze in bas-relief representing the three temptations of Our Lord Jesus Christ in the desert.

Lesson 64

The Vices or Capital Sins

The soul, like the body, has weaknesses and illnesses. It has inclinations that carry it toward sin: these are what the catechism calls vices.

The first is pride. We see this sin in a parable of the Gospel: a Pharisee entered the Temple to pray, he put himself in a good place and said: "O God, I give Thee thanks that I am not as the rest of men, extortioners, unjust, adulterers....I fast twice a week: I give tithes of all that I possess." And seeing a Publican in the Temple, standing afar off and praying, saying: "O God, be merciful to me, a sinner," the Pharisee added: "I give Thee thanks I am not like this Publican."[77]

Notice that this man had an exaggerated self-esteem; he did not see his faults, but only spoke of his qualities, a disposition which made him prefer himself to everyone else. He had committed a sin of pride.

---

[77] Luke 18:10-14

However, God does not like prideful men, and He rejected the prayer of the Pharisee, whereas He accepted that of the humble Publican.

Jesus gave this advice about avarice: "Take heed and beware of all covetousness: for a man's life doth not consist in the abundance of things which he possesseth." And

He spoke a parable to them, saying: "The land of a certain rich man brought forth plenty of fruits. And he thought within himself, saying: 'What shall I do, because I have no room where to bestow my fruits?' And he said: 'This will I do: I will pull down my barns and will build greater: and into them will I gather all things that are grown to me and my goods. And I will say to my soul: Soul, thou hast much goods laid up for many years. Take thy rest: eat, drink, make good cheer.'" But that very night, God required his soul of him.[78]

REVIEW – To what could you compare vices? – Show that the Pharisee committed a sin of pride. – What did Jesus say about greed?

LESSON

- 427. *What is a vice?*

A vice is a defect or a bad inclination which draws us to sin.

---

[78] Luke 12:15-20

† 428. *How many principal vices are there?*

There are seven principal vices: pride, covetousness, lust, envy, gluttony, anger, and sloth.

> NOTE: These vices are called "capital sins" because they are the source of most sins.

429. *What is a prideful man?*

A prideful man is one who boasts of his qualities, as though they came from him, and who despises other people.

430. *What is a miser?*

A miser is one who is too attached to all that he possesses and in particular to money.

431. *What is a lustful man?*

A lustful man is one who willfully lets his mind wander toward impure thoughts or desires, or lets his eyes wander to bad looks, or who says impure words, or commits impure actions alone or with others.

432. *What is an envious man?*

An envious man is one who is saddened at the good of others or who rejoices at their misfortunes.

433. *What is a glutton?*

A glutton is one who eats or drinks to excess for the sole pleasure of eating or drinking.

> NOTE: The most dangerous form of gluttony is drunkenness, which makes one lose his reason,

The Vices or Capital Sins

makes a man resemble a beast and finally leads to alcoholism. Alcoholism ruins a man's health and does a great deal of harm to the family and to society.

434. *What is an angry man?*

An angry man is one who flies into violent rages against people, animals or things.

435. *What is a slothful man?*

A slothful man is one who does not want to work or who works without vigor.

> FOR MY LIFE – There are certain sins which I commit more easily than others. This is because they have at their source a bad inclination, perhaps a vice. I will seek this source of my dominant fault and make it known to my confessor.
>
> PRAYER – "I renounce sin and the occasions of sin, especially those into which I often have the occasion of falling."
>
> THE WORD OF GOD – "Whosoever committeth sin is the servant of sin." (John 8:34)

LITURGY – Artists sometimes represented the capital sins in cathedral sculptures.

ASSIGNMENT – Do you know a parable in which Jesus condemned pride? – Do you know one in which He condemned avarice? – Did not Jesus become angry when He chased the money-changers from the Temple? Why? – Is it a bad thing to be lazy?

CATECHISM FOR CHILDREN

PROJECT – Illustrate using dioramas, clay models or stages with moveable characters, the parables of the Pharisee and the Publican, of the workers in the vineyard, of the foolish virgins, etc., in which Our Lord condemned certain vices; or else the parable of the cockle and the wheat, in which He explained God's conduct toward the wicked.

LESSON 65

THE DAY OF A CHRISTIAN

LESSON

436. How may a day be spent in a Christian manner?

A day may be spent in a Christian manner by offering to God all that I do, and by doing nothing which displeases Him.

† *437. What should you do when you wake up?*

When I wake up, I should make the sign of the cross and say: "My God, I give You my heart."

† *438. What should you do when you are dressed?*

When I am dressed, I should say my morning prayer on my knees.

- 439. *What will you do to sanctify your work?*

To sanctify my work, I will offer it to God and I will do my best, putting all my heart and effort into what I am doing.

- 440. *What should you do before and after your meals?*

Before and after my meals I should say a brief prayer or at least make the sign of the cross.

441. *What is it good to do when you hear the bell ring morning, noon and evening?*

When I hear the bell ring morning, noon and evening, it is good to recite the Angelus.

- 442. *What should you avoid in your games and your leisure?*

In my games and my leisure, I should avoid everything which would be contrary to purity and charity.

> NOTE: Games and leisure are indispensable means of recreation, but they should not last longer than the proper time.

443. *What should you avoid in your conversations?*

In my conversations I should avoid speaking badly of my neighbor, lying and saying vulgar things.

- 444. *What should you do when you are tempted to offend God?*

When I am tempted to offend God, I should ask Him for the grace not to offend Him.

> NOTE: You can say these words of the "Our Father": Our Father, lead us not into temptation.

† 445. *What should you do when you have committed a sin?*

When I have committed a sin, I should repent for having done it, ask forgiveness of God and promise to go to Confession as soon as I can.

446. *How should you accept the painful things which happen to you?*

I should accept the painful things which happen to me with submission to the will of God, and I should offer them to Him in reparation for my sins and for the sins of others.

† 447. *How should you end the day?*

I should end the day with the evening prayer and an examination of conscience.

> NOTE: Truly Christian families say the evening prayer together; this pious practice maintains families in the faith and draws down upon them the blessings of God.

> **FOR MY LIFE** – I will ask my confessor for a rule of life, that tells me how often I should go to Confession or receive Communion, what sacrifices I should make, on what point I should focus my efforts, etc.
>
> **PRAYER** – "My God, I offer You my actions of this day; grant that they may always be according to Your holy will, for Your greater joy."
>
> **THE WORD OF GOD** – "My yoke is sweet and My burden light." (Matthew 11:30)

ASSIGNMENT – In your opinion, what is necessary in order to be a good Christian?

PROJECT – Draw a filmstrip illustrating each of the Beatitudes with some picture of a Saint; or else make a leaflet on the life of Saint Francis of Assisi or Saint Theresa of the Child Jesus.

Lesson 66

Revelation and the Bible

Jesus said: "Blessed are they who hear the word of God and keep it." (Luke 11:28)

We therefore have to listen to God Himself in order to reach the happiness which has been promised to us.

God spoke to men by the prophets of the Old Testament and especially by His Son Jesus.

Jesus gave His Apostles the responsibility of transmitting His teachings to us.

Read the account of the mission of the Apostles. (Matthew 28:16-20)

LESSON _____

448. *How do we know the truths of religion?*

We know the truths of religion from God Himself, Who revealed them to us.

> NOTE: The body of truths which God Himself made known to men is called Revelation.

449. *By whom did God reveal to man the truths of religion?*

God revealed to man the truths of religion by the prophets of the Old Testament, by His Son Jesus Christ and by the Apostles.

450. *Where do we find the truths which God has revealed?*

We find the truths which God has revealed in Holy Scripture and in oral Tradition.

451. *What is Holy Scripture?*

Holy Scripture is the Word of God written under His inspiration; we also call it the Bible.

452. *What is oral Tradition?*

Oral Tradition is the teaching which the Apostles received from Jesus and which they have transmitted to the Church by word of mouth.
"I am with you all days, even to the consummation of the world." (Matthew 28:20)
"Lord, to whom shall we go? Thou hast the words of eternal life." (John 6:69)

REVIEW – What is Revelation? – How did Jesus, the prophets and the Apostles prove that they were speaking in the name of God? – How has the teaching of God been kept intact all the way down to us? – What do you know about mysteries? – What is the Bible? – Recite the Act of Faith.

LESSON 67

THE HOLY BIBLE

Long before Jesus came upon the earth, God spoke to men through the prophets. These put in writing the revelations which God had made to them.

Before ascending into Heaven, Jesus commanded His Apostles to transmit His teaching to men.

The Apostles first preached by word of mouth; then a few of them put into writing the principal teachings of Jesus.

The whole of the books inspired by God, written before and after Jesus Christ, form the Bible.

Through the Bible, it is God Who is speaking to us. The Bible is therefore the Word of God; it cannot deceive us in the teachings which it gives to us.

Read the Prologue of the Apocalypse; Jesus reads and explains the Bible (Luke 4:16-22).

453. What are the two parts of the Bible?

The two parts of the Bible are the Old Testament and the New Testament.

454. Of what is the Old Testament composed?

The Old Testament is composed of books of the Bible written before the coming of Jesus.

> NOTE: The books of the Old Testament are extremely varied. Some tell the history of the People of Israel; others are collections of laws or prayers; others contain the writings of prophets or wise men; all are meant to prepare the full revelation of the New Testament.

455. Of what is the New Testament composed?

The New Testament is composed of books of the Bible written after Jesus Christ: these are the four Gospels, the Acts of the Apostles, the Epistles, and the Apocalypse.

> NOTE: The books of the New Testament which we should know above all are the four Gospels; they contain the life and the teachings of Jesus.
>
> Their authors are Saint Matthew, Apostle; Saint Mark, disciple of Saint Peter; Saint Luke, disciple of Saint Paul; and Saint John, Apostle.

Prayers

Our Father (The Lord's Prayer)

Pater noster, qui es in caelis, sanctificetur nomen tuum; adveniat regnum tuum; fiat voluntas tua, sicut in caelo et in terra.

Panem nostrum quotidianum da nobis hodie; et dimitte nobis debita nostra, sicut et nos dimittimus debitoribus nostris; et ne nos inducas in tentationem; sed libera nos a malo. Amen.

Our Father, Who art in heaven, hallowed be Thy name; Thy kingdom come; Thy will be done, on earth as it is in heaven.

Give us this day our daily bread; and forgive us our trespasses, as we forgive those who trespass against us; and lead us not into temptation, but deliver us from evil. Amen.

Hail Mary (The Angelic Salutation)

Ave Maria, gratia plena, Dominus tecum, benedicta tu in mulieribus, et benedictus fructus ventris tui, Jesus.

Sancta Maria, Mater Dei, ora pro nobis peccatoribus, nunc et in hora mortis nostrae. Amen.

Hail Mary, full of grace, the Lord is with thee. Blessed art thou among women, and blessed is the fruit of thy womb, Jesus.

Holy Mary, mother of God, pray for us sinners, now and at the hour of our death. Amen.

The Apostles' Creed

I believe in God, the Father Almighty, Creator of heaven and earth, and in Jesus Christ His only Son, Our Lord; Who was conceived by the Holy Ghost, born of the Virgin Mary, suffered under Pontius Pilate, was crucified, died and was buried; He descended into hell and on the third day He rose again from the dead; He ascended into heaven and is seated at the right hand of God, the Father Almighty; from thence He shall come to judge the living and the dead.

I believe in the Holy Ghost, the holy Catholic Church, the Communion of Saints, the forgiveness of sins, the resurrection of the body, and life everlasting. Amen.

THE CONFITEOR

I confess to Almighty God, to blessed Mary ever Virgin, to blessed Michael the Archangel, to blessed John the Baptist, to the holy Apostles Peter and Paul, to all the Saints, (and to thee, Father,) that I have sinned exceedingly in thought, word and deed, through my fault, through my fault, through my most grievous fault. Therefore I beseech blessed Mary ever Virgin, blessed Michael the Archangel, blessed John the Baptist, the holy Apostles Peter and Paul, all the Saints, (and thee, Father,) to pray to the Lord our God for me.

ACT OF FAITH

O my God, I firmly believe that Thou art one God in three divine Persons, the Father, the Son, and the Holy Ghost; I believe that Thy divine Son became Man, and died for our sins, and that He will come to judge the living and the dead. I believe these and all the truths which the holy Catholic Church teaches, because Thou hast revealed them, Who canst neither deceive nor be deceived.

ACT OF HOPE

O my God, relying on Thy infinite goodness and promises, I hope to obtain pardon of my sins, the help of Thy grace, and life everlasting, through the merits of Jesus Christ, my Lord and Redeemer.

Act of Charity

O my God, I love Thee above all things, with my whole heart and soul, because Thou art all good and worthy of all love. I love my neighbor as myself for love of Thee. I forgive all who have injured me and ask pardon of all whom I have injured.

Act of Contrition

O my God, I am heartily sorry for having offended Thee, and I detest all my sins because I dread the loss of heaven and the pains of hell, but most of all because they offend Thee, my God, who art all good and deserving of all my love. I firmly resolve, with the help of Thy grace, to confess my sins, to do penance, and to amend my life. Amen.

Memorare

Remember, O most gracious Virgin Mary, that never was it known that anyone who fled to thy protection, implored thy help or sought thy intercession was left unaided. Inspired by this confidence I fly unto thee, O Virgin of virgins, my Mother. To thee do I come, before thee I stand, sinful and sorrowful. O Mother of the Word Incarnate, despise not my petitions, but in thy mercy hear and answer me. Amen.

SALVE REGINA

Salve Regina, mater misericordiae; vita, dulcedo, et spes nostra, salve. Ad te clamamus, exsules filii Hevae. Ad te suspiramus, gementes et flentes in hac lacrimarum valle. Eia ergo, advocata nostra, illos tuos misericordes oculos ad nos converte. Et Jesum, benedictum fructum ventris tui, nobis post hoc exsilium ostende. O clemens, o pia, o dulcis Virgo Maria.

Ora pro nobis, sancta Dei Genetrix. Ut digni efficiamur promissionibus Christi.

Hail, holy Queen, Mother of Mercy, our life, our sweetness and our hope. To thee do we cry, poor banished children of Eve. To thee do we send up our sighs, mourning and weeping in this valley of tears. Turn then, most gracious advocate, thine eyes of mercy towards us, and after this our exile show unto us the blessed fruit of thy womb, Jesus. O clement, O loving, O sweet Virgin Mary.

Pray for us, O holy Mother of God. That we may be made worthy of the promises of Christ.

PRAYER OF THE ANGEL AT FATIMA

My God, I believe, I adore, I trust, and I love Thee! I beg pardon for those who do not believe, do not adore, do not trust, and do not love Thee.

Most Holy Trinity, Father, Son and Holy Ghost, I adore Thee profoundly. I offer Thee the Most Precious Body, Blood, Soul, and Divinity of Our Lord Jesus Christ, present in all the tabernacles of the world, in reparation for the outrages, sacrileges, and indifference by which He is offended. And through the infinite merits of His Most Sacred Heart and the Immaculate Heart of Mary, I beg of Thee the conversion of poor sinners.

THE REGINA CAELI

Regina caeli, laetare. Alleluia.
Quia quem meruisti portare. Alleluia.
Resurrexit sicut dixit. Alleluia.
Ora pro nobis Deum. Alleluia.
Gaude et laetare, Virgo Maria. Alleluia.
Quia surrexit Dominus vere. Alleluia.

Oremus.

Deus, qui per resurrectionem Filii tui Domini nostri Jesu Christi, mundum laetificare dignatus es: praesta, quaesumus, ut per ejus Genitricem Virginem Mariam, perpetuae capiamus gaudia vitae. Per eumdem Christum Dominum nostrum. Amen.

Queen of Heaven, rejoice! Alleluia.
For He Whom you were worthy to bear, alleluia,
Has risen as He said, alleluia.
Pray for us to God, alleluia.
Rejoice and be glad, O Virgin Mary, alleluia.
For the Lord has truly risen, alleluia.

Let us pray.

O God, through the resurrection of your Son, our Lord Jesus Christ, you were pleased to make glad the whole world; grant, we beseech you, that through the Virgin Mary His mother, we may obtain the joys of eternal life. Through the same Christ Our Lord. Amen.

LORD JESUS, TEACH US TO BE GENEROUS

Lord Jesus, teach us to be generous.
Teach us to serve You as You deserve,
To give without counting the cost,
To fight without worrying about wounds,
To labor without seeking rest,
To sacrifice ourselves without expecting any other reward,
Save that of knowing that we are doing Thy holy will. Amen.

PRAYER ATTRIBUTED TO SAINT FRANCIS OF ASSISI

Lord, make me an instrument of Thy peace.
Where there is hatred, let me sow love;
Where there is injury, pardon;
Where there is discord, harmony;
Where there is error, truth;
Where there is doubt, faith;
Where there is despair, hope;
Where there is darkness, light;
Where there is sadness, joy.
O Divine Master, grant that I may not so much seek to be consoled as to console.

PRAYER TO JESUS CRUCIFIED

(To obtain a more intense Faith, Hope, Charity, and contrition for our sins.)

Behold, O kind and most sweet Jesus, I cast myself upon my knees in Thy sight, and with the most fervent desire of my soul I pray and beseech Thee that Thou wouldst impress upon my heart lively sentiments of faith, hope and charity, with true repentance for my sins and a firm desire of amendment, whilst with deep affection and grief of soul I ponder within myself and mentally contemplate Thy five most precious wounds, having before mine eyes that which the Prophet David spoke of Thee, O good Jesus: "They have pierced My hands and My feet; they have numbered all My bones." (Psalm 21:17-18)

THE ANGELUS

The Angel of the Lord declared unto Mary.
And she conceived by the Holy Ghost.
Hail Mary...
Behold the handmaid of the Lord.
Be it done unto me according to thy word.
Hail Mary...
And the Word was made flesh.
And dwelt among us.
Hail Mary...
Pray for us, O holy Mother of God.
That we may be made worthy of the promises of Christ.

Let us pray. Pour forth, we beseech Thee, O Lord, Thy grace into our hearts, that we to whom the incarnation of Christ Thy Son was made known by the message of an angel may, by His Passion and Cross, be brought to the glory of His Resurrection. Through the same Christ Our Lord. Amen.

PRAYER TO THE VIRGIN MARY

Holy Mary, Mother of God,
Preserve in me the heart of a child,
Like a fountain limpid and pure.
Obtain for me a simple heart,
Which does not relish sadness;
A heart magnanimous in gift of self,
Tender in compassion;
A generous and faithful heart,
Which forgets no good deed,
And is bitter at no evil;
Form a meek and humble heart in me,
Loving without asking in return,
Joyful to disappear in another heart,
In the Heart of Your divine Son.
A great and unconquered heart,
Straitened by no ingratitude,
Wearied by no indifference;
A heart tormented for the glory of Jesus Christ,
And wounded by His love,
Of a wound to be healed only in heaven.

TO SAINT JOSEPH

Saint Joseph, Guardian of virgins and father to whose faithful care Christ Jesus, innocence itself, and Mary, Virgin of virgins, were entrusted, I ask and beg of thee, through these two dearest pledges, Jesus and Mary, preserve me from all defilement, and make it always possible for me, unsullied in mind, pure in heart, and chaste in body, to give to Jesus and Mary my holiest service. Amen.

BEFORE MEALS

Bless us, O Lord, and these Thy gifts, which we are about to receive from Thy bounty, through Christ Our Lord. Amen.

AFTER MEALS

We give Thee thanks, Almighty God, for these and all Thy benefits, who livest and reignest forever. Amen.

THE ROSARY

"A family that prays is a family that is alive." (Pius XII)

"I am Our Lady of the Rosary. I have come to ask you to say the rosary every day and to change your life…"

(The Blessed Virgin at Fatima, October 13, 1917)

How to Recite the Rosary

Reciting the rosary is praying to God through Mary.

Reciting the rosary is thinking with Mary about the life of Jesus.

Begin by making the sign of the cross.

Next, recite the "I Believe in God": it is a summary of the truths which God taught us about Himself and about the way He came to earth, lived here, died, and rose again to allow us to go to heaven with Him.

Then say an "Our Father," three "Hail Marys" and the "Glory Be to the Father," which is a homage of love and adoration to the Holy Trinity.

Next recite the five decades.

After the "Glory Be," one can also add the short prayer which the Blessed Virgin taught to the children of Fatima:

"O my Jesus, forgive us our sins; save us from the fires of hell; lead all souls to heaven, especially those most in need of Thy mercy."

These prayers are known around the world and are recited by children as well as by grown-ups.

During each decade, we meditate alongside Mary an event from the life of Jesus. Through the joys, the sufferings and the glory of her Son, she shows us the great love of Jesus, Who always did the will of His Father; he reveals to us by His obedience that He is truly God made man, and our model.

The meditation of the different mysteries gives to well-disposed and attentive souls the graces which Jesus and Mary earned by their actions full of love.

Every Christian should have a rosary and carry it with him. We can recite the rosary, or simply a decade, at any moment of the day, even if our hands are busy with other things. We are always sure to please the Blessed Virgin.

The Joyful Mysteries: meditated Monday and Thursday

1. The Annunciation: for humility
2. The Visitation: for love of our neighbor
3. The Nativity: for the spirit of poverty
4. The Presentation in the Temple: for purity and obedience
5. The Finding of Jesus in the Temple: to seek God's will in all things

The Sorrowful Mysteries: meditated Tuesday and Friday

1. The Agony in the Garden: for a greater sorrow for sin
2. The Scourging at the Pillar: for the mortification of our senses
3. The Crowning with Thorns: for the forgiveness of our evil desires
4. The Carrying of the Cross: for the acceptance of our sufferings.
5. The Crucifixion and Death of Jesus: for a greater love of God and of souls

The Glorious Mysteries: meditated Wednesday, Saturday and Sunday

1. The Resurrection of Jesus Christ: to believe in the love of God

2. The Ascension: for the desire of heaven

3. The Descent of the Holy Ghost upon Mary and the Apostles: for the descent of the Holy Ghost in our souls

4. The Assumption of the Most Blessed Virgin Mary: for the grace of a happy death

5. The Crowning of the Most Blessed Virgin Mary Queen of Heaven and Earth: for an ever greater devotion to Mary

VISIT TO THE MOST BLESSED SACRAMENT

After Mass, Jesus is still there in the church. A lamp which is always burning tells us that Jesus is present.

Thus, at every hour of the day, we can come to make a visit and adore Him.

Come and kneel before Jesus present in the tabernacle.

I. ADORE

Adore Jesus Who is God and Who accepts to be present in the form of the host, for our sake.

Pray in silence for a moment...

II. GIVE THANKS

Thank God for a few moments

- for being there to hear you;
- for all of the graces He gives you.

Pray in silence for a moment...

III. ASK

Ask Jesus for everything you need: He listens to you like a friend.

- Above all, ask to be a saint;
- pray for your family and your friends;
- pray for the Church, the Pope, and the priests.

Visit to the Most Blessed Sacrament

Pray in silence for a moment…

IV. Make reparation

Make up for the pain which your sins and all sins have caused Jesus. Jesus is a friend; He wants you to be present here to love Him and console Him. Perhaps you do not love Him enough… and so many people do not love Him at all!

Pray in silence for a moment…

"My God, I believe, I adore, I trust, and I love Thee! I beg pardon for those who do not believe, do not adore, do not trust, and do not love Thee."

"Most Holy Trinity, Father, Son and Holy Ghost, I adore Thee profoundly. I offer Thee the Most Precious Body, Blood, Soul, and Divinity of Our Lord Jesus Christ, present in all the tabernacles of the world, in reparation for the outrages, sacrileges and indifference by which He is offended. And through the infinite merits of His Most Sacred Heart and the Immaculate Heart of Mary, I beg of Thee the conversion of poor sinners."

Do not forget to end with a prayer to the Blessed Virgin.

The Sacrament of Penance

To receive the sacrament of Penance well, you must know your sins, have contrition for them, accuse yourself of them, and, after receiving absolution, do the penance given by the priest.

What is it to go to Confession? It is to say your sins to a priest in order to receive absolution.

How do we go to Confession?

There are two things to do: remember our sins and be sorry for them.

In order to remember them, we should say slowly:

Holy Ghost, – the light of our hearts, – enlighten my conscience, – show me my sins, – make me see them, – as I will see them at the hour of judgment, – and as Jesus saw them, – when He was dying to make reparation for them. – Show me the reasons why I committed them, – so that I may fight against them. – Grant me the firm resolution to follow the advice of Thy priest, – so that Thy grace may encounter fewer obstacles in me, – and may heal me of my wicked inclinations. – Amen.

Then closing our eyes let us think of our sins. We can use the following examination of conscience to help us remember:

Examination of Conscience

1. Our Previous Confession

• How long has it been since my last Confession? Did I tell all of my sins?

• Did I willfully *hide* any serious sins? (If yes, you absolutely must accuse yourself of having done so, for not only were none of your sins forgiven which you confessed, but you added another very serious sin called a *sacrilege*.)

• Did I *forget* any serious sins? (If yes, your last Confession was still good, but you must accuse yourself of them now.)

• Did I prepare myself badly for my last Confession?

• Did I lack sorrow for my sins? That is to say, true repentance? (To have true repentance, one must be determined to do everything possible no longer to commit them.)

• Did I say my penance?

• What resolution did I make at my last Confession? Did I keep it?

2. The Commandments of God

First commandment:

I am the Lord thy God, thou shalt not have strange gods before Me.

• Did I fail to say my prayers? Morning prayers, evening prayers? Often?

• Did I say my prayers badly? (For example, not kneeling down when I could have done so.)

- Did I shorten my prayers? Omit the evening examination of conscience?
- Was I ashamed to appear Christian?
- Did I speak against religion?
- Has it been a long time since I received Communion, simply by neglect?

Second commandment:

Thou shalt not take the name of the Lord thy God in vain.

- Have I used foul language?
- Have I sworn?
- Have I taken oaths for little or no reason?

Third commandment:

Remember thou keep holy the Lord's day.

- Did I miss Mass on Sunday or a holy day of obligation by my own fault? How many times?
- Did I arrive late? At what part of the Mass?

Fourth commandment:

Honor thy father and thy mother.

- Have I disobeyed my parents?
- Have I talked back to my parents? To my teachers?
- Did I make fun of them?
- Did I pout or act sullen?
- Did I make sarcastic comments?

Fifth commandment:

Thou shalt not kill.

- Have I argued with others?
- Have I hit anyone?
- Have I held a grudge?
- Have I sought revenge?
- Have I given a bad example or drawn others to sin?

Sixth and ninth commandments:
Thou shalt not commit adultery.
Thou shalt not covet thy neighbor's wife.

- Have I looked at bad or impure pictures? Have I looked for impure magazines on purpose?
- Have I watched bad shows (on television, for example)?
- Have I participated in bad conversations? Was I the ringleader?
- Did I commit any impure actions? Alone? With others?

Seventh and tenth commandments:
Thou shalt not steal.
Thou shalt not covet thy neighbor's goods.

- Have I taken or tried to take anything which was not mine (candy, money, other objects)?
- Have I purposely damaged what did not belong to me?
- Have I cheated at games? Have I copied other students' work in class, on a test, on an assignment, on my homework?

Eighth commandment:
Thou shalt not bear false witness.

- Have I lied (for fun, to show off, to get out of being punished, to deceive others)?
- Have I lied in order to have others punished?
- Have I thought ill of others without sufficient reason?
- Have I been indiscreet? Or curious? Have I tried to find out other people's secrets?

3. The Commandments of the Church

- Did I prepare myself well for my last Communion?
- Did I receive Communion without having fasted?
- Have I received Communion with grave sin on my conscience?
- Have I eaten meat on days I should not have?

4. The Capital sins

- Have I sinned by *pride?* Have I refused to admit that I was wrong? Have I despised others in my thoughts? Have I been boastful? Have I been irritated over nothing? Have been too particular or too vain in my way of dressing?
- Have I sinned by *gluttony:* by being too picky? by eating and drinking to excess? Have I smoked in secret?
- Have I sinned by *avarice?* Have I refused to lend my things?
- Have I been *jealous?*
- Have I become *angry?* Have I been moody, making life difficult for those around me? Have I intentionally tried to make others angry?

- Have I been *lazy?* In waking up in the morning? In praying? In receiving Communion? In doing my homework? Have I missed school or catechism class by my own fault?
  - My dominant fault is: ...
  - I resolve to: ...

If you are afraid of forgetting your sins, write them on a paper (without putting your name) which you will destroy after going to Confession.

Now that you have thought of your sins, before you tell them to the priest, you have to regret them with all your heart, or else you will not be forgiven.

IN THE CONFESSIONAL

When you go in, say to the priest: "Bless me, Father, for I have sinned. It has been (however long) since my last Confession."

Then say your sins: "Father, I confess to having done..., I confess that I..." When you have finished accusing yourself of your sins, say: "I am sorry for these and all the sins I have forgotten."

Answer any questions the priest may have and listen to his advice.

Say the Act of Contrition while the priest gives you absolution.

Act of Contrition

O my God, I am heartily sorry for having offended Thee, and I detest all my sins because I dread the loss of heaven and the pains of hell, but most of all because they offend Thee, my God, Who art all good and deserving of all my love. I firmly resolve, with the help of Thy grace, to confess my sins, to do penance, and to amend my life. Amen.

After your Confession

We must say the prayers, or do the things which the priest gave us as a penance, as soon as possible.

We should decide what efforts we will make to live a better life, asking God to help us. Let us confide our life and our resolutions to the Blessed Virgin, our Mother.

THE HOLY SACRIFICE OF THE MASS

The Mass is the Sacrifice of the Cross made present upon the altar. It is the most important act in the life of a Christian. Only the sacrifice of Jesus saves us from our sins and allows us to go to heaven.

Mass is the best means for us to honor God. It unites us to the most holy Person of Jesus and to His sacrifice.

A Christian who understands well what is the Mass is happy to assist at it often, and even every day, if it is possible.

On Sunday, the Church obliges us to go to Mass. We would seriously offend Our Lord if we did not unite ourselves to His sacrifice; it would be a grave sin.

"The Ordinary of the Mass"

The prayers which one says at every Mass are called the "Ordinary of the Mass" (you can find them in the middle of most missals).

| I. Preparation | Prayers at the foot of the altar
Kyrie
Gloria
Epistle
Gospel
Creed |
|---|---|
| II. Offertory | Offering of the host
Offering of the chalice
Lavabo |
| III. Consecration | Sanctus
Canon of the Mass |
| IV. Communion | Pater Noster
Agnus Dei
Communion of the priest
Communion of the faithful
Last blessing
Last Gospel |

"The Proper of the Mass"

Every Sunday, and almost every day, has a special feast with its own prayers. They are called the "Proper of the Mass."

These feasts belong:

• either to the Temporal Cycle, which is above all the sequence of Sundays. In this way, we follow the life of Christ through the course of each year. (The Temporal Cycle is usually at the beginning of the missal.)

• or to the Sanctoral Cycle, when we celebrate nearly every day the feast of one of the Saints. Certain feasts are even holy days of obligation (the Immaculate Conception, the Assumption, All Saints' Day). (The Sanctoral Cycle generally comes after the Ordinary.)

The prayers of the Proper are: Entrance hymn (Introit), Collect, Epistle, Gradual and Alleluia, Gospel, Offertory hymn, Secret prayer, Communion hymn, Postcommunion prayer.

Indulgences?
missals?
Jews?
Apocrypha?
Latin?
Mary?
Pentecost?
Apostolic Succession?
Purgatory?
Communion of Saints? saints?
Holy lands?
Pope Leo XIII vision?
Easter duty?
do my penance? fasting?
which level clergy are you?